Once Upon a Time in Seattle

#516

Emmett Watson

Introduction by Mary Daheim

Foreword by William L. Dwyer

Kenmore, WA

NORTH
WEST
CORNER
BOOKS

Northwest Corner books, an imprint of Epicenter Press Inc., publishes reprints of out of print titles about the Pacific Northwest. For more information, visit www.EpicenterPress.com

Cover and interior design: Aubrey Anderson

ISBN: 978-1-941890-24-0 (Trade Paperback)
ISBN: 978-1-941890-25-7 (Ebook)

Library of Congress Control Number: 2018949827

Originally published in 1992 by Lesser Seattle Puiblishing.
Published by arrangement.

This book is for Betty Watson, Nancy Brasfield and Lea Watson, natives and loved ones all.

Contents

Introduction

From tinker to tailor and back again, Emmett Watson has captured the disparate personalities of the people who have made Seattle into the cosmopolitan yet still laidback city we locals all love to call home. Frankly, I'm sure Watson probably loathed what was happening here in his later years since he famously beat the drums for what he called Lesser Seattle.

But that takes nothing away from how much he loved this city and how keenly he observed its inhabitants. For old natives like me, the people he wrote about are as familiar as the rain. From the Foreword by his old pal U. S. District Court Judge William L. Dwyer to the saints and the sinners, Watson wrote about them all. With his puckish sense of humor in place, he could both cheer and chastise.

He'd started out as a baseball player—a catcher. But that career didn't last long. He would overcome polio in adulthood and end up writing for all three of Seattle's major dailies, which included the *Seattle Star* with its pink front page and ultimate demise in 1947. Watson moved on to the *Seattle Post-Intelligencer* and finally the *Seattle Times*.

As I read through his book, I recognized almost all of the names. One was of nationally-known golfer Harry Givan, who had gone to Lincoln High School with my Aunt Frances. She had a crush on Harry, but it wasn't reciprocated. I went to Lincoln with Harry's daughter, Sharon. I mention this because of Watson's uncanny knack for making his readers feel you not only knew him, but all of the people he was talking about—including the ones you didn't know. I was lucky—I got to meet Watson at a book event on Queen Anne Hill. In person, he seemed like an ordinary guy. In print, he loomed like a giant.

—Mary Daheim,
author of the Alpine and Bed-and-Breakfast mystery novels
March 2018

Foreword

There never will be another book about Seattle like this one. Emmett Watson brings to life men and women of times past who made the city what it is, or who just had some fun and left us a legacy of laughter. Watson, it must be said, has been around long enough to have known many of these people personally.

In the twentieth century Seattle has changed from a frontier town to what is called, these days, a world-class city. The march of progress is not entirely gratifying to the author. "Every time a Columbia Center goes up," he writes, "a price must be paid on the sidewalk." He remembers fondly when life on low-rise Union Street, with its cheap cafes and pool halls, small hotels and barber shops and shoeshine stands, "could provide one with a baccalaureate in street smarts; it was a trade school of interpersonal values, a cement campus of camaraderie."

Seattle was blessed in those days with men and women who were generous or tough or funny or brilliantly inventive or some combination of these, and who would be unforgettable—except that we forget everything, in a generation or so, without a storyteller to keep memory fresh.

These are some that Watson tells about:

- Nick Foster, the amiable young radio operator who served the Northwest's biggest bootlegging ring and went on, years later, to start up educational TV on Channel 9.
- Roy Olmstead, the police-lieutenant-turned-bootlegger whose prosecution inspired a great dissent by Justice Louis Brandeis of the United States Supreme Court.
- Elsie Olmstead, Roy's charming, cultivated, polyglot wife, the hostess of the rum-running headquarters.
- George Vanderveer, the famous criminal defense lawyer, as devoted to street-brawling as to the art of cross-examination.

- Bertha K. Landes, Seattle's only woman mayor to date, and one of its best, the forerunner of the many women now in local government, who fired a corrupt chief of police and routed, for a time, a complacent male establishment.
- A brave nine-year-old boy named George Weyerhaeuser, whose kidnapping for ransom became a legend of the Northwest.
- Harry Givan, whose effortless mastery of golf inspired Bing Crosby to say, "I could take him through Texas with a bag of clubs, a chuck-a-luck game, and a balloon dancer, and we'd have all the money in the state."
- Al Rochester, a school dropout who became one of the city's best-loved politicians and opened the door to the Seattle World's Fair.
- George Pocock, the genius of crew racing and shell building, his eccentric predecessor Hiram Conibear, and their oarsmen, who first put the University of Washington on the nation's athletic map.
- Terry Pettus, prosecuted as a political radical, shunned for years and consigned to poverty, who "lived to witness his own redemption," saved the houseboat community, and became a hero of the city.
- Meyer Rothstein, who relished being called "Jew Mike," operated an honest second-floor gambling establishment, and could lose 70,000 Depression-era dollars on the turn of a single card with no apparent regret.
- Chairman Bill Allen, test pilot Tex Johnston, and others who led Boeing out of its post-war doldrums and into world leadership in aerospace, transforming the company's home town in the process.

Many others appear in these pages—tycoons, politicians, athletes, lawyers, engineers, gamblers, reporters.

Emmett Watson himself could have filled a chapter in this book if someone else had written it. In his time he has been a professional baseball player (a catcher, stout of heart but so slow of foot that fans reportedly would get up a card game waiting for him to round third base), one of the few surviving airplane pilots who is both deaf and absent-minded, the proprietor for many years of the city's most famous newspaper column, and the founder of a mythical organization called Lesser Seattle, Inc., which claims 283,475 members according to figures he makes up as he goes along. Watson is as much a monument of the city as the Pioneer Square totem pole.

Seattle is becoming a high-tech place, and if forecasts are right it will grow into an ever bigger, richer, more paved-over and more crowded city. But let us not forget where we came from. We are reminded of earlier and simpler days by fishermen casting from waterfront docks, weeds cracking through neighborhood sidewalks, spacious frame houses with back yards, wooden telephone poles, old office buildings with windows that can be opened, wild blackberry bushes that keep probing for territory no matter what, parks and open spaces, the mountains in plain sight, the fresh and salt water all around. And we are reminded also by Emmett Watson's book, which brings back colorful Seattle people from what seems like just the other day.

—William L. Dwyer,
July 1992

Killing the Monster

At exactly 12:58 p.m., June 27, 1992, with no witnesses present, I killed the monster. The corpus delicti, the physical evidence, is in your hand. There will be no apology for this misfeasance.

The "monster" comes out of a quotation I once read by Winston Churchill:

"Writing is an adventure. To begin with, it is a toy and an amusement. Then it becomes a mistress, then it becomes a master, then it becomes a tyrant. The last phase is that just as you are about to be reconciled to your servitude, you kill the monster and fling him to the public."

Never in my wildest, euphoric fantasies would I ever compare what I do with what Mr. Churchill did in the matter of writing. But there is a similarity. A book does begin as fun, then increasingly it becomes a burden, then it becomes dictatorial and overbearing. Finally, you get it over with and kill the monster.

It cannot be said too often, although many have tried, that writing is solitary work. But any writer who says that producing a book is done solely by the author is an egomaniac or a charlatan, probably both.

It took a lot of people to help write this book many did not know they were helping. But they were, and I am grateful. The writing began in October 1991, so it was nine months in the making. But what went into the book came from a lifetime of living in Seattle, back to the evening, perhaps, when I heard my father first utter the words, "Big Bertha."

I must have interviewed a hundred people for the stuff included here. At least it seems like that many. Of course, a lot of it had nothing to do with "interviewing," not in the formal sense. It came from being around, just hanging out, so to speak becoming ever more fascinated by some of the people who contributed to the history of Seattle.

The Northwest is singularly blessed in having good writers. Not many regions have a historian like Norman Clark, whose books are a shining record of what it was like to live around here. I relied heavily on his book *The Dry Years*, a history of Prohibition in Washington state, for the chapter on Roy Olmstead. Mr. Clark was gracious with his time for a personal interview.

The late Ralph Potts deserves special mention. On social occasions he first awakened my interest in Olmstead, the bootlegger, and in George Vanderveer. Ralph's book *Counsel for The Damned*, written with Lowell S. Hawley, was a valuable resource on the great Seattle attorney.

Earl and Charyl Sedlik were kind enough to invite me into their home on Ridgeway Place in Mount Baker, for reasons that will become apparent as we go along. The Sedliks' generous hospitality is deeply appreciated.

Junius Rochester was most helpful. Even though I knew his father, Al Rochester, well, Junius was of great assistance and read the chapter on his father for accuracy.

To Charley McIntyre, Stan Pocock and Vic Forno go my thanks for the chapter on George Pocock and Washington crew. I also used material from the late Gordon Newell's fine book *Ready All*, a history of Northwest rowing. That book, by the way, was conceived and sponsored by the late H. W. Mccurdy.

Susan Stanley was a wonderful cheerleader when the going got tough. But more important, it was Susan who got me interested in Terry Pettus; she gave me valuable assistance and urged upon me the notion, since confirmed by my own friendship with Terry, that he was indeed a great man.

In addition to my own prowling, the stuff on Union Street and Jew Mike came mainly from Dottie Venable, who was a hostess for so long at the Magic Inn. The boxing manager George Chemeres also gave me several hours of his time.

An old friend and sports department colleague, Vincent O'Keefe, gave me much help in reviewing earlier days at the *Seattle Times*, where I am now kept in a stable and fed regularly. He gave me some genuinely human insights into the colorful Johnny Dreher. I would also like to thank Henry MacLeod, former managing editor of that paper, who made the entire Weyerhaeuser kidnapping chapter possible. It was my good luck that Henry kept a large and exciting scrapbook on that long-ago period.

The chapter on Boeing was in many ways the hardest but the most pleasurable to write. Research on this chapter led me to the acquaintance of Jack Steiner and Joe Sutter. These two men were giants in the building of airplanes. Also, most helpful were Paul Spitzer, the Boeing historian, and Shery Nebel, a talented dynamo in Boeing's public relations department. A bow of thanks, as well, to Carl Cleveland, head of Boeing public relations in the exciting days of the Dash-80.

I relied on several excellent books done by Boeing people. Among them are *Boeing in Peace and War* by E. E. Bauer and *The Road to the 707*, by William H. Cook. Jack Steiner's own carefully crafted and detailed book, *Jet Aviation Development: One Company's Perspective*, was a valuable tool in getting a handle on that very complex subject.

Steiner gave generously of his time for personal interviews. So, did Joe Sutter, popularly known at Boeing as "the father of the 747."

Also valuable were many private conversations with my friend the test pilot Tex Johnston. His own book, *Tex Johnston: Jet-Age Test Pilot*, is a classic in its field.

One other book on Boeing is *Legend and Legacy*, a lively, readable and anecdote-packed history of the company. Not a dry line in a car load. Legend and Legacy came out in June 1992, and I was lucky to make the acquaintance of the author, Robert J. Serling, one of the nation's premier aviation writers. Serling, an upbeat, pleasant fellow, was most generous with his time and expertise. To anyone interested in this unique Seattle company, I wholeheartedly recommend Serling's book.

Without Nancy Hevly, my own book might never have been completed. Nancy is a woman of almost supernatural editing talent. When she said something must go, it went. When she rearranged paragraphs, they looked much more presentable. She was terrific.

The people in the *Seattle Times* library were patient and helpful. I would especially like to thank Steve Selter, Patti Leahy, Lorraine George and Sandy Freeman.

The awful job of early, first-draft manuscript reading fell to Jim Halpin, himself a writer of surpassing ability. He was unfailingly kind, and our friendship survived this delicate relationship. I also drew on a long-standing friendship with Carol Barnard, who freely offered counsel at appropriate times.

Every writer could use a brutal sergeant like Lejeune of *Beau Geste* ("Keep shooting, you scum, and you'll get a chance yet to die with your boots on"). My own Sgt. Lejeune was Fred Brack, an editor and business head who exhorted, organized, criticized, propped me up in the parapets and literally forced me to kill the monster.

In passing, I would like to thank the Seattle Mariners for the free pass they gave me to their press box. Part of the book was scribbled there with a pen on the back of a lineup card during dull periods of their games. Now and then the Mariners would absent-mindedly load the bases with Junior Griffey coming up. At that point, all literary pretensions were put aside.

Other parts of this book were scribbled down in rough notebook form on the second bench you come to upon entering Myrtle Edwards Park. In addition, I once scribbled a paragraph on a paper towel in the men's room of Rosellini's 910.

I would also like to thank my dog, Tiger, a runt miniature poodle. He is a friend and counselor whose olfactory excellence includes sniffing at bad prose. At his suggestive sniffs, some rewriting was necessary.

In looking back over the characters in this book, it occurs to me that they all had in common a singular strain of individuality. None were all good or all bad. Each had an air of independence, and most had a quality of toughness that made them both admirable and interesting.

Growing up in Seattle, I have often counted myself lucky for being raised by a working-class family. My dad dug basements for a living, using a team of horses and a large scoop shovel. One of his hired hands was a jocular, rough-hewn fellow named David Adams, whom we called Dady.

In addition to working for my dad, Dady was rather typical of Northwest working men. He worked in logging camps and in sawmills, almost anything that involved hard labor; he swore freely, used snoose and drank more than his share. I vividly remember the "tin pants" he wore in winter. These were, almost literally, tin pants; they were heavy and water-repellent, necessary protection if you worked outdoors in Seattle weather. When Dady climbed out of his tin pants they were stiff enough to stand alone.

As a kid, my first job was in a sawmill at Selleck, a settlement not far from Black Diamond. One of my tasks was rolling logs and "feeding the slip" on the mill pond. The fact that I couldn't swim was never thought to be a handicap.

In those early years, during and before college, I worked at Boeing, at Todd Shipyard, at the Seattle-Tacoma Shipyard and later as a longshoreman. I still have my longshoreman's lethal-looking metal cargo hook in a drawer by my bedside. I have also worked in the orchards around Wenatchee and Chelan, where I "thinned 'cots" for twenty-five cents an hour.

The point in setting this down is that I really got to know the kind of people who made Seattle a great place in which to grow up. These hard-working men were kindly, helpful and tolerant of a kid with no skills or any great shakes of a work ethic. You could learn from them.

I remember once working in the hold of a ship as a longshore "permit man" while going to the University of Washington. I was young then, full of radical ideas and the kind of self-righteousness that passes itself off as idealism.

During a pause in the loading, we had time to talk. On this particular occasion, a veteran longshoreman friend filled me in on what the waterfront was like during the bloody strikes of 1934. He talked about the hostile cops, the strikebreakers, the bitterness and violence of those benighted days. I said, "They were all sonsabitches, weren't they?"

My friend laughed. "Yeah, kid, they were sonsabitches, all right," he said, "but at least they were OUR sonsabitches."

As I grew older, I came to realize that there was a lot of Seattle in that remark. As this book demonstrates, Seattle was a city with a rough, raw past; a place of corruption; a waterfront crossroads town; a city tucked away in the far Northwest. We had our full share of sonsabitches, but we did not suffer outsiders gladly.

As I learned more about Seattle's rugged, undisciplined past, its payoffs, its palms-out officials, its lousy, no-good, rotten politicians, I began to wonder why the city stayed so uniquely ours. It was a place where prostitution, gambling and bootlegging were rampant. Except for occasional spasms of civic reform, it was a difficult, even dangerous, place to be. And I wondered why, in this ripe atmosphere, there never has been a hint of organized, syndicate crime—the kind that prevailed, and still prevails, in Eastern cities, and in Chicago and Kansas City.

I got a hint of why this is so one time when I was talking to Ernie Yoris, chief of detectives with the Seattle police department. Ernie was strong, tough and smart—well qualified to be what he was. And Ernie told me what happened one time in the 1930s. He said there were a half-dozen Chicago hoods holed up at the old Olympic Hotel. The Seattle cops knew they were there. The cops also concluded that they had come in to case the city, to find out what might be done with some well-organized, mob-dictated discipline.

The way Ernie told it, there were no niceties about civil liberties to consider. After talking it over with his cohorts, Ernie just picked up the telephone and called the head hood.

"Get your asses out of this town," he said. "You've got 30 minutes to check out and be on your way. If you aren't gone by then, we're coming up there and bust some heads."

Ernie said things like that happened now and then. He said Seattle was too nice a place to have the likes of them around.

Of recent times a myth has sprung up about Seattle, propagated by the hundreds of magazine and newspaper profiles on the city. The myth goes: "Seattle is such a friendly city, the people are all so nice to visitors." That may be true, in a sense. But my friend Jonathan Raban, the premier British essayist, who came here, looked around, and then decided he liked Seattle better than any city in the world, puts quite a different spin on the myth.

"Seattle is not an overly friendly city," he said. "It is a civil city, but not altogether friendly. People from outside mistake the civility for friendliness. Seattle is full of people who have their own lives to live. They won't waste their time being friendly. But they are civil."

The roots of modern Seattle came out of labor strife, the "bosses" vs. "us," and indeed the working class of this city was quite radical. The International Workers of the World flourished here. So, did Anna Louise Strong, who later became one of the best-known communists outside Russia. Seattle is the only large city in America ever to have had a general strike. It is no accident that Dave Beck, a Seattle labor leader, became one of the nation's most powerful men.

In his book on President Wilson, *When the Cheering Stopped*, Gene Smith describes the President's visit to Seattle. I have never read anything like it. As Smith describes it, the Wilson party made its way up Second Avenue to cheering throngs along the sidewalk. It was after World War I, and Wilson was popular.

"He was standing up in the car waving a high silk hat ... when with terrifying suddenness all the noise and cheering ended. Standing by the curb in long lines were men in blue denim working clothes. Their arms were folded, and they stared straight ahead, not at the President but at nothing at all. They did not hiss or boo but motionless, noiseless, simply stood there."

They were members of the IWW—the International Workers of the World. Their Seattle home, if they had any, was the Skid Road, where they hung out, gave speeches, drank and gambled. They were radicals, and they were protesting what they called the Wilson administration's treatment of "political prisoners" during World War I.

"For six blocks the statue-like men lined the street. When the car had gotten past the silent, terrible blocks there were more cheering people, but the President did not again rise in the car; he simply waved his hand and weakly smiled."

This incident proves, I suggest, that not all Seattle citizens in all times were friendly and welcoming. Many working men, it can be assumed, were not IWW members; to cover six blocks on both sides of the street required many more Wobblies than even Seattle could provide.

Earlier I mentioned Dave Beck, a man who is the unique, the quintessential individualist of Seattle. He was a small boy here. He delivered newspapers on First Hill and down into the Skid Road. He cadged free lunches in the saloons. Because he was very poor and needed to help his mother to support him, he shot rats for bounty under the University Bridge. He would have no truck with radicals; he liked business people better. But he was a tough, spirited man, shaped by his years as a boy on the streets of Seattle.

He first led the Seattle Teamsters, then led the West Coast Teamsters, and, finally, became head of the International Teamsters—a power in both labor and American politics. When Beck needed to embrace the Washington, D.C. political precincts (what is now called "The Beltway"), he took an entourage of Seattle people with him.

Among these was my late friend Guy Williams, himself a product of Northwest logging and shingle mills. As Guy described it, the idea was to present Beck to the Eastern sophisticates and power brokers as a man of the world, a man of vision.

"The whole idea blew apart, Guy told me, "when Dave showed up at our first big presentation. He was wearing his Elks badge prominently in the lapel of his suit, and he told everybody how proud he was to have been the Exalted Ruler of the Seattle Elks Lodge 92. He was proud of that, and he didn't care who knew it."

While Beck's Teamsters were powerful and, in some ways, corrupt, they were also clear of mob influence. Unlike Detroit, New York and other large Teamster enclaves, there were no racketeers in Beck's Seattle labor movement. Beck was a uniquely moral man in many ways and he was always a booster for Seattle. He did not tolerate outsiders well.

A true story concerns the time that Bugsy Siegel, the gangland killer, came to Seattle to see Beck about some minor union matter at his Flamingo Hotel in Las Vegas. Siegel arrived in Beck's outer office unannounced. At the time, Dave had a wonderful secretary, a very pretty woman named Ann Watkins. Something about Bugsy Siegel's presence bothered Ann—it was said that Bugsy, very much the ladies' man, took the occasion to lay his attentions on her.

Ann rang a buzzer under her desk. Just as Beck appeared from his own office, three burly Teamsters arrived. Without a word, they went over and picked Siegel up and slammed him to the floor. Shaken and white, Bugsy got back to his feet. Then he said, half in admiration, "Jesus, you guys play rough."

"Yes, when we have to," Beck said. "Now get out of here and don't come back."

LOOKING OVER THESE CHAPTERS, I insist that the people in them had in common a certain toughness, a Northwest element of individuality.

I hope that some of the toughness, the individuality found in the characters in this book survives today. Seattle is still a good city, replete with people of strength and character, creativity and brains. No matter how much it becomes gentrified or adopts the passing fads of this late twentieth century, the city is still uniquely its own, one of a kind.

I can think of no other place quite like it.

1

The Baby Lieutenant

Nick Foster, an angular young man, was a radio operator on the *Jefferson*, a tidy, somewhat ornate wooden ship that made tourist runs between Seattle and Skagway. There were six or seven radio operators hanging around Seattle's waterfront, Nick being one of them. Nick was now out of work because it was late summer, 1924, and there would be no more runs to Alaska. Nick always tried to find a ship that had a good cook, so he would especially miss the *Jefferson* because it had comfortable quarters and the food was great.

As a radio operator Nick made $70 a month. When he departed the *Jefferson*, he went uptown and rented a small sleeping room with a hot plate in it, and he made some phone calls, letting it be known that he was in the market for another ship. Early in September Nick got a call from Mr. 0. R. Redfern and this alarmed him, because 0. R. Redfern was supervisor of Puget Sound radio for the Federal Communications Commission, and if he found any radio infractions he could put you on the beach for good.

"There is a job available right now," Mr. O. R. Redfern said, "but I want to tell you something about this job. You can be the engineer for a radio station. I can't tell you much more about it, except that the station broadcasts out of a home in the Mount Baker district.

"This radio station is run by some people who are thought to be rumrunners. So, I want you to be careful. You should keep your radio license available at all times. If anything happens, it can identify what you are hired to do. Don't let yourself get caught on any kind of infraction. This could be a touchy job, but it may be all right. Why don't you go look at it?"

1

Nick hopped on a streetcar and found the right address in Mount Baker, which was 3757 Ridgeway Place. It was four blocks east of Franklin High School. The place was really more a mansion than a house, two stories, on a double comer lot, large manicured lawns, a pond in the back, located on a quiet street overlooking Lake Washington.

Nick felt a few shakes as he went up the walkway and knocked on the front door. He heard steps inside and when it opened a large fellow filled the doorway. He was about 6 feet 2 inches tall, not fat, but bulky and square-set, a very handsome man with a big smile, and Nick remembered thinking that this man could charm a bird out of a tree. Nick knew right away that he was looking at "the baby lieutenant," a genuine Northwest legend.

"Come in," the man said. "I am Roy Olmstead."

Nick took an instant liking to Roy Olmstead. The reason they called him the baby lieutenant" was because of Roy's rapid rise in the Seattle Police Department. He had joined the police force in 1906, and his chief, Austin Griffiths, called him "upright, bright and competent." Starting as a harness bull, he had advanced through the ranks during some of the most violent years in Seattle history, under such mayors as Hiram Gill, George Cotterill, Hiram Gill again, and finally "Holy Ole" Hanson. By 1910, only four years on the force, Olmstead became a sergeant and in 1916 he was promoted to lieutenant. He was 26.

As Roy gave him a tour of the house, Nick noted his soft-spoken way of talking, his easy assurance. Roy's wife, Elsie, came downstairs and Nick began to understand a little more about the refinement evident in every room. Elsie was a bright, vivacious lady who spoke several languages. She was from Liverpool by way of Vancouver, B.C., and she had filled the house with expensive, imported furniture, in harmony with the wood paneling. She told Nick the paneling was Australian gumwood. Nick admired the wall hangings and the thick, expensive draperies. In a way, he felt out of his comfort zone.

But the Olmsteads made him feel at home. Roy and Elsie took him up the wide, circular staircase to the second floor, showed him the master bedroom with built-in shelves and walk-in closets. Another bedroom, on the southwest corner, was almost as large as the master bedroom. Both rooms opened onto a sundeck. The second bedroom was filled with transformers, microphones and radio equipment. This was the headquarters of one of Seattle's first and most powerful radio stations, KFQX.

To run a radio station, you had to have a licensed operator on the job, one of whose duties was to maintain a watch on ship frequencies in Puget Sound. By law you made sure the broadcast station did not interfere with an SOS call or some other form of ship communication. The Olmsteads explained this to Nick and said he should come to the house in the late afternoons. The station's assigned broadcast hours began at 6:30 p.m. with news reports, weather information and stock market quotations. It went off the air at 9 p.m.

Roy and Elsie sat Nick down at a large, highly polished, Italian-made table in the dining room. Elsie served a pot of tea and some finger sandwiches with the crusts removed, each sandwich good for about one bite. He was not offered anything else to drink. He noticed there was no smoking in the Olmstead house. Elsie radiated good cheer and energy. She said she intended to make KFQX the best radio station in the Northwest. Later, she said, she would do her broadcasts from a downtown studio in the L. C. Smith Tower. Then she told Nick about Aunt Vivian.

Aunt Vivian was the star at KFQX and Aunt Vivian was, of course, Elsie Olmstead. She read bedtime stories to Seattle's children. The show was already popular because the children liked Elsie's well-modulated voice and her English accent. She read the children bedtime stories and recounted fables. Sometimes she read them the newspaper comic strips.

Roy told Nick that the radio station had been put together by a young man named Alfred M. Hubbard, some kind of a mechanical whiz, whom Roy obviously liked. Hubbard had been the station's original operator. He was only one of Roy's many employees.

So, Nick left that evening with a job. He boarded a Mount Baker streetcar and went back downtown to his furnished room with the hot plate in it. He sat on the edge of the bed and reflected on his good fortune—a steady job, a lovely working environment, nice people, good pay, easy hours and free finger sandwiches. Nick didn't much like tea, but that was bearable.

Then he thought about 0. R. Redfern and what he had said: "They are rumrunners. So, I want you to be careful. You should keep your radio license available at all times. Don't let yourself get caught on any kind of infraction. This could be a touchy job..."

Prohibition, the Volstead Act, was in force, sort of. all across the United States gangs were running liquor in from Canada. There was moonshine and bathtub gin, and a whiff of some of this stuff would make a mule walk backward. Rumrunning and moonshining brought on gang warfare; there were hijackings and there were killings. Police were corrupted by the big money and so were federal enforcement agents. Prohibition lawlessness was rampant in Chicago, Detroit and other large cities. Killings were routine because turf was important and profits enormous. The big names in liquor were Dion O'Banion and a crude, bull-necked mobster named Al Capone, head of a large smuggling and moonshining empire in Chicago that reached the East Coast and on down to Florida.

As the weeks went on with Aunt Vivian and Roy Olmstead, Nick Foster was learning more about his benefactors, and the more he learned the better he liked them. He would be at the Mount Baker mansion and he would see Elsie Olmstead giving away food, sometimes clothing, to people without money. She did it, he noticed, with warmth and good humor, without condescension. He also became aware that he was working for two Seattle celebrities.

Aunt Vivian became ever more popular on KFQX. When he was downtown, Nick would sometimes buy children's books for Elsie, so she could read them aloud when she came on the air at 7:15. There was a constant stream of visitors to the Olmstead home because Roy was so well liked in Seattle. He knew politicians, all of Seattle's ranking police, several former mayors, many of the city's successful businessmen.

People stopped to talk to Roy when he went downtown, and his name was dropped in the exclusive Arctic Club. He was on very friendly terms with the mayor, Edwin (Doc) Brown, who in private life was a "painless" dentist and was reputed to be a gifted sculptor of false teeth. Roy knew the police chief, Bill Severyns, particularly well, and among the people who liked to chat with him was William E. Boeing, who ran a growing airplane company out on the Duwamish.

The historian Norman Clark, whose book *The Dry Years* is the definitive work on Prohibition in Washington state, cited a news clipping that described Roy's status in the community:

"Public officials, professional men, merchants and bankers waved cheery greetings to him. Twenty men would speak to him in one block on Second Avenue. He had the power that goes with good liquor, easy to get, and good money, easy to give. He was the toast of parties where popping corks warmed the gregarious spirit …. a bootleg king?… It made a man feel important to casually remark, 'As Roy Olmstead was telling me today …' "

There were people who would not have been surprised if Olmstead had been invited to address the downtown Rotary.

Roy had been in business four years when Nick first came to his house in Mount Baker. He had made bootlegging reliable, even respectable, in Seattle. The city seemed to bask in his lawbreaking, and businessmen who did not like Prohibition would say of him, "Roy is a force for social good."

When he was still on the police force, being regarded as the boy wonder of Seattle law enforcement, Roy impressed even judges with his obvious intelligence; he had a sense of responsibility, according to Norman Clark, and he would frequently appear in court to recommend fair sentencing, even probation, for certain miscreants. Judges began to defer to his recommendations. It got around that a word from Olmstead was useful and might even get a man off. Here is where he first crossed the line, when he weighed integrity against the cash that criminals and their attorneys were willing to pay him for his influence with the courts. As Clark has pointed out, "Olmstead had to face the true nature of his ambition."

Introspection on one's ambition is usually a quiet matter. Selling your influence can be handled over a friendly cup of coffee. But the true nature, the real magnitude, of Olmstead's ambition became very public on the early morning of March 22, 1920. It exploded into newspaper headlines the next day. On a dark, lonely beach at Brown's Bay, not far from Edmonds, Roy and some of his friends were caught unloading cases of illegal liquor from a tugboat. Prohibition agents had been waiting there for several nights. Lights flared in the 2 a.m. darkness and agents began firing on the tugboat. As men scurried about, shouting, and the tug headed full bore for open water, Roy jumped into his car and escaped. But he was recognized by the agents, and they had now taken possession of what Clark called "the largest shipment of liquor ever seized in the Northwest."

Olmstead was arrested that same afternoon. He was instantly suspended from the police force, then arraigned on a federal charge, released on bail, and ultimately fined $500. Well, hell ... a minor setback. Now free of the time-consuming job of being a model career officer, Roy went into liquor smuggling in a big way. Soon it was discovered that the "baby lieutenant" was far more than just another errant cop who had wrecked his career with one fatal misstep.

Roy set about revolutionizing the entire haphazard, badly overcrowded enterprise of rumrunning. In the next few years, there would not be a businessman in Seattle, any devotee of the fine arts of free enterprise, who would fail to admire Roy's talent for administration and organization.

To get started he needed capital. So, he persuaded eleven investors to put up $1,000 apiece. He assembled a staff. It included boatmen, salesmen, bookkeepers and dispatchers. He hired good mechanics on Lake Union to service his fleet of swift boats. He made contacts in Canada and hired ships out of Vancouver to stop at D'Arcy Island to unload whiskey, which was transferred to the smaller boats that made their speedy runs down Puget Sound.

To profit from the Volstead Act, Canada slapped a duty of twenty dollars a case on liquor bound for the United States. Roy hired ships cleared for Mexico, where no duty applied. He got discount prices because he ordered liquor in such large quantities; now he could undersell rival rumrunners by as much as 30 percent. Some of Roy's competitors were driven out of business; some turned to piracy; and a few joined Olmstead. At the peak of his operations, Roy had some 90 employees delivering $200,000 worth of liquor in Seattle every month. He even acquired a small freighter and leased a beachfront farm to handle deliveries. His operations extended down the coast to Oregon and into California. His volume was so great he went into wholesaling.

Roy's deliveries were steady and reliable. He produced good bonded stuff, name brands like Glenlivet, Usher's Green Stripe and Old Smuggler. Only quality liquor, thanks to Roy Olmstead, went into Seattle's better-known speakeasies, like the Bucket of Blood in Pioneer Square, the Boulevard Inn, just off Interlaken Avenue, Doc Hamilton's place up on Twelfth Avenue, the Black and Tan at Twelfth and Jackson, and, of course, the Rose Room, which was the city's social center, in the Butler Hotel at Second and James. A lot of illegal drinking went on in Chinatown, in Georgetown, out on 85th and Greenwood; in Belltown, there seemed to be a speakeasy at every other door.

Roy's people delivered directly to many of Seattle's most distinguished private homes, the houses of businessmen, lawyers, teachers and, to be sure, judges. The city's prestigious private clubs were never without the best. Roy knew exactly whom to take care of in the Seattle police department; some of his deliveries were carried in a police motorcycle sidecar.

There was an aura of adventure about Olmstead. He often went out himself on his booze-running soirees. He picked nights of rain and wind and darkness, terrible weather which, he knew, would keep federal agents and hijackers off the waters. On some occasions, in broad daylight, his crews would make deliveries on the city's busy downtown waterfront, the liquor transferred to small trucks with signs painted on them: "Fresh Meats, Sausages, Hams," "Lettuce and Cabbages" and "Occidental Bread."

Federal Prohibition agents were underbudgeted and underpaid. They were forced to use Coast Guard boats or almost anything they could rent. They always trailed Roy's swifter boats: the *June*, the *Comet*, the *M22* or the *Eva B*. Roy had a larger one built to order, powerful and fast, with an all-black hull, which he christened the *Elsie*. Olmstead's chief worry was not the police, or the federal Prohibition agents, or the Coast Guard. His immediate dangers came from the hijackers, the pirates of Puget Sound. These were dangerous people who engaged in open gunfights on the waters and beaches. Even if attacked, Roy's boats never fired back.

Olmstead abhorred violence. None of his runners, dispatchers or boatmen were allowed to carry guns, and frequently he would lecture them to this effect: "Nothing we do is worth a human life." He never cut nor diluted his liquor—always the straight, good stuff—and it was beneath his dignity to deal in moonshine. Because people did not care for Prohibition, and perhaps because of it, drinking was a delicious novelty. People carried booze to parties in flasks and even in hot water bottles. To many Seattleites, the former baby lieutenant had become "the honest bootlegger." There is no mystery to how Roy Olmstead became Seattle's most romantic figure.

The members of Olmstead's efficient, well-controlled gang had some marvelous nicknames: Captain Hat, Eddie the Pup, Short Card Johnson, Scrap Iron. By nature, some were lawless, even ruffians, yet to a remarkable extent Roy kept his people under control. He had an innate air of authority, and because he was tall, erect, almost military in bearing, they referred to him as The Major or The Commander.

So, the money rolled in, all cash, and that is how Roy and Elsie Olmstead came to live in that splendid Mount Baker mansion. When Nick Foster met him, Roy was four years into the business of providing Seattle with the best liquor.

Sometimes in the hot late summer of 1924, Nick Foster would report for work and find Roy sitting on the edge of the small pond next to the mansion soaking his feet in the cool water. As weeks passed they got to,be friends and Nick became almost a member of the Olmstead household. From the beginning, Nick knew that there wasn't a drop of liquor in the house. The king of Northwest rumrunners would not allow liquor in his home.

Years later Nick would recall, "A riotous evening was sitting at the kitchen table as Elsie talked about her background in England. She came out of the Liverpool area in the fall of 1919. Her real name was Elise, but everyone called her Elsie. She had worked in the army recruiting services in Liverpool for about three years, came to Vancouver in 1920. Roy had been married, two children, but he was divorced, and he married Elsie early in 1924."

They were devoted, Roy and Elsie, and you could not think of a more idyllic existence; plenty of money, trips to Europe for Elsie, a regular cook and a housekeeper, as well as a gardener to keep up the grounds. The gardener was a fixture on Roy's payroll because sometimes he delivered the good stuff to Roy's neighbors. But mostly he worked on lawns and shrubs, and because he immersed himself in a lot of fresh fertilizer you sometimes could smell the gardener as far away as Franklin High School.

Elsie enjoyed being Aunt Vivian. She was committed to the station and saw it as becoming a full-time business if the Volstead Act, heaven forbid, were ever repealed. She hoped that one day the station would make the Olmsteads truly respectable and elevate her and Roy into the middle class, the upper part of it.

People in Seattle fastened onto the notion that the children's stories Elsie read in the evenings were laced with code words to tell Roy's boatmen where to bring in the liquor to be loaded on trucks.

This notion, this rumor of code words salted into children's stories, came to be accepted. But Nick knew it was nonsense. Being a radio expert, he knew there were many better and more reliable ways of contacting the rumrunning crews. Besides, Elsie didn't know what she was going to say until Nick, monitoring the KFQX transformer, handed her the children's stories. He picked the stories to be read and marked them, knowing how long it would take her to read each one. As for the rumrunning operations, the deliveries were ordered by telephone from the mansion or from downtown. Roy had reliable help, but a lot of the movement, the day-to-day strategy, was directed by Olmstead himself from Mount Baker. Roy had installed nine telephone lines in the big house on Ridgeway Place.

Without being part of the liquor dealing, Nick was still considered a trusted ally in the Olmstead empire. The Commander liked him. But still, Nick kept his radio license fastened to the wall above the transformer, remembering what Mr. O. R. Redfern had told him.

One of Olmstead's people even took Nick over to a house on Beacon Hill one day, the house in which the Olmstead ring kept the money. There was a huge safe in the basement and Nick was allowed downstairs he didn't see any money.

One evening after tea and finger sandwiches, Nick boarded the streetcar and went back downtown to his sleeping room with the hot plate in it. It had rained that evening and Nick was tired and wet. When he switched on the overhead light in his room he was startled to see a man sitting on his bed. The man told Nick not to be alarmed, that he worked for the government. The manager had let him into Nick's room, he explained.

"You are pushing the 18th Amendment, aren't you?" Nick said.

"Yes," the man said, "I am with the alcohol division, and we would like to find out some things about the house in Mount Baker. Like who comes and goes there, who Olmstead talks to. You'd be smart to help us."

Nick said, "I am a licensed radio operator. I am only there in an official capacity and I don't know anything about what goes on there. I monitor the transformer, I do what I am supposed to do."

Finally, the man from the alcohol division left. The next day, when he came to work, Nick told The Commander what had happened. The news didn't bother Roy at all. "Don't worry about it, Fos," Roy told him.

As the evenings went on, Nick Foster saw more of the federal agents. Sometimes two of them would be waiting in his room when he arrived home and they would fire more questions at him. Relying totally on his official capacity, that of a licensed radio operator, Nick continued to tell them he knew nothing of Roy's private business. This went on for a while and finally he talked to Olmstead again, and Roy said, "How often do they come, Fos?"

Nick said, "They come quite often, and I am getting tired of it." "Don't worry about it, Fos, nothing will come of it," Roy said. The Commander was very relaxed.

Meanwhile, Nick had come to know Roy's bagman. The bagman's name was Bennett, but Nick never learned his first name. Bennett had a wife, a very pretty woman, who came to the house quite often. Elsie liked the wife and had even taken her to Europe on one of her trips. Together they visited France, Italy and Spain, exploring the museums and eating at the best restaurants.

The bagman, an affable fellow, was only about 5 feet 4 inches tall. He was a fashion plate. He wore carefully tailored suits, always a tie, sometimes even spats, and Nick began to think of him as Mr. Dapper himself.

Mr. Dapper also wore a long black overcoat with a velvet collar, a coat that came down almost to the floor. He visited the house at irregular intervals. It appeared that the bagman's function was to collect the cash, take it to the safe on Beacon Hill, and arrange its distribution to people who otherwise would become critical of Roy's enterprise. One night, after Nick had monitored Aunt Vivian in the upstairs broadcasting studio, he flipped the station off the air and came down the circular staircase and went into the kitchen. What he saw made him pause, almost in embarrassment, like a man who has inadvertently walked into the ladies' room. There, clustered around the large kitchen table, were Roy, Aunt Vivian and the dapper bagman.

On the table were stacks of big denomination bills. Nick had never seen so much money—stacks of tens and twenties, pads of fifties, pads of hundreds. While the trio counted the bills, they carried on a casual conversation. When the counting was done the bagman opened his long black coat, and Nick saw that it was specially cut and tailored with many pockets inside to carry these packets of bills. As he watched Mr. Dapper, Nick thought, "This guy must be bulletproof with all that padding. That coat must weigh fifty pounds."

And when the short man with the long black coat said good night, he went out the door, climbed into his car—a red Stutz Bearcat—and, Nick was sure, drove over to the house on Beacon Hill. There would be one of Roy's agents in the house where they kept the money. He and the little bagman would go downstairs and open one wall, which could be moved lengthwise, like a boxcar door, and behind this door was the safe, the centerpiece of the Olmstead rumrunning industry. The little man would empty his coat, packet by packet, and stack the bills in the safe.

That night when Nick went home, he was glad he did not have visitors in his room. He was beginning to learn more than he wanted to know about the business of keeping Seattle in liquor.

But a couple of nights later, the agents were back and waiting. There were two of them, and they were persistent. What went on at the Olmstead house? Who was there last night? Any drinking going on? How many phones?

The visits continued. The dry agents began to tell Nick more than he was telling them.

Gradually Nick became aware that his persistent visitors worked for Roy C. Lyle, the administrator, for the 20th District of the Prohibition Service, part of the Treasury Department. Lyle's district covered Washington, Oregon and Alaska. He had been appointed by Senator Wesley L. Jones. His skill at pursuing rumrunners and bootleggers had been honed by his previous careers as real estate salesman and librarian. In other words, he was something of a joke.

Lyle was considered to be rather slow on the uptake, and his principal function, it seemed, was to please the Anti-Saloon League forces on behalf of Senator Jones.

The real work was done by William M. Whitney, Lyle's legal adviser and chief assistant. The historian Norman Clark later summed up

Whitney by saying that, while Whitney was "energetic and untiring," he was sometimes indiscreetly direct and ruthless.

"Even by 1922," Clark has written, "he had offended so many people around Seattle by searching the automobiles and homes of solid citizens and by his ax and hammer methods that the Seattle Star urged that he be fired."

Because the pay was poor, Whitney's agents were a scruffy lot. These undercover Prohibition enforcers had been accused of all kinds of crimes, from taking bribes to sadism to whoremongering—even murder. One of Whitney's agents, the notorious "Kinky" Thompson, a brute and a bully, was killed in a brawl with a Tacoma policeman. Thompson had been widely feared. He pistol-whipped prisoners, beat up women, and, as Nick Foster later recalled, "when the patrolman emptied his .45 into Kinky, there was some serious talk in Tacoma about putting up a monument to him."

The agents waiting in Nick's sleeping room became more threatening. They told him he would land in prison if he didn't cooperate. Nick began to feel tormented. His feelings toward Roy and Elsie were now so warm that the battle between fear and loyalty was tearing him up inside. He had nobody to tum to except The Commander himself, and Nick told Roy everything the agents were saying.

Nick did not know how many of the nine telephones in Roy's house were tapped. "But there is no two ways about it," he told Roy, "they have tapped at least two of them. They told me that last night. They also told me that they are definitely going to raid this house."

The Commander had a low opinion of Lyle and Whitney and their agents. He knew all about the wiretaps. On lines he was sure were tapped, he would give false directions to the boats; it gave him exquisite pleasure to know that the agents, and perhaps Whitney himself, were shivering on some wet beach, waiting all night to capture a speedboat full of liquor that never came. And on some of these calls, Roy would insult Whitney with scorn, calling him a bumbler and a fool. "Anytime I can't outwit that damn fool Whitney, I don't belong in this business," Roy said over one tapped line.

Being an ex-cop, Olmstead had great confidence in his knowledge of law and the rules of evidence. He was convinced that, if it ever came to a trial, Whitney's wiretaps would be useless. The court would not permit tapped phone conversations to be admitted as evidence. There was even a Washington state statute, adopted in 1909, that made wiretapping illegal. Roy also knew that if a raid on his Mount Baker home ever did materialize, the agents would come up with nothing in the way of liquid evidence, since he and Elsie banned liquor on the premises. So, Roy listened to Nick telling him about the threatened raid and he replied: "Aw, Fos, don't let that bother you. They would never in the world get around to raiding this place.

"Don't worry about it, you worry too much. No wonder you are skitty. Come on, let's go in the kitchen and have some tea. Forget it."

Early in November Mr. Dapper came again, wearing his floor-length black coat with the velvet collar. Nick was not present when they counted the big denomination bills on Olmstead's kitchen table, but he was there when Bennett said goodnight. He watched as Bennett went out the front door and started up his red Stutz Bearcat. His long coat was full of money. The money spread him out in all directions, making him look even shorter than he really was, and Nick remembered thinking that when Mr. Dapper left, he looked like a stuffed teddy bear.

That is the last anyone ever saw of Mr. Dapper. He did not drive to the house on Beacon Hill that had the safe in its basement. He was gone. By the next day it became apparent that nobody would hear from him again and there was a great deal of caterwauling and crying as Elsie tried to console Mr. Bennett's distraught, abandoned wife. Quite possibly he had been robbed and murdered, but more likely Olmstead's reliable courier, his trusted bagman, was now somewhere in British Columbia, across the U.S. border, probably heading east in his Stutz Bearcat. Mr. Bennett was a Canadian citizen and, before joining Roy, had once worked as a banker in Canada.

Being one of the nation's top bootleggers, used to dealing in great amounts of cash, Roy had developed a kind of resigned fatalism about the corrosive effects of money on a man's loyalty. Most of his gang were loyal—he paid them top wages—and the police were reliable, too. There was no instance where any of the policemen became dishonest by arresting one of Roy's men. They stayed bought. But the defection of his bagman hit Roy hard. Nick noticed that Roy became very quiet, keeping to himself for several days, until it finally sank in that he had about a $300,000 hole in his cash flow and a trusted aide speeding away in a Stutz Bearcat.

Roy looked rich and he acted rich, but the overhead in rumrunning was high. Prohibition agents, tapping one of his phones, heard a Seattle policeman complain that Roy was not doing enough for the motorcycle boys. "Jesus Christ," Roy said, "It is split so many ways now that I am broke. When I get through, there is nothing left."

But life went on placidly at Ridgeway Place and the evening of November 24, 1924, seemed no different from any other. Al Hubbard, Roy's mechanical wizard, dropped by for a visit. The cook was busy in the kitchen. Nick Foster took one of the children's books, marked up some of the stories for Aunt Vivian to read, and settled in to monitor the transformer. Mrs. Bennett, having somewhat recovered from grieving about her departed husband, was there. Earl Gray, the orchestra leader at the Butler Hotel, had come for dinner. Dinner being over, Roy and Hubbard were in the master bedroom with the day's newspapers spread out on the bed.

Nick hunched down before the radio transmitter as Aunt Vivian went on the air. It was about 7:30.

As Nick concentrated on the transformer, he felt something cold on his neck. He turned around to find himself looking at the barrel of a .45 automatic, fully cocked and held by a large man with whiskers, whose clothes were covered with mud and dirt. The man was holding the .45 in both hands.

"Turn that thing off," the man said.

Nick reached up, flipped a switch, and radio station KFQX went off the air forever. The unkempt visitor motioned him ahead and walked Nick down the elegant circular stairway to the entrance hall, then to the living room, and, finally, into a scene of absolute bedlam. Five more tough-looking, mud-dirty characters, all carrying sawed-off pump shotguns, had the Olmstead household under guard. In charge of these mean-looking, low-rent agents was William Whitney, legal adviser and assistant to Prohibition administrator Roy Lyle, who was there too. Whitney was a short man, rather dumpy, and like his agents, he was tracking mud over Elsie's expensive carpet.

Nick was frightened and appalled. To make matters more loudly chaotic, Whitney had brought his wife along on the raid. This man, a federal agent, had brought his WIFE along! She seemed to be in a semi-hysterical state of triumph and she kept screaming, "We got 'em! We got 'em!" Elsie Olmstead had blown a gasket and she rushed to a telephone to call the police. Whitney grabbed the phone from her hand and pushed Elsie away. The agents began ransacking the house for evidence, because without evidence, you had nothing much going in the way of a raid. The men with shotguns herded everybody into the living room and Whitney and his wife began using the Olmstead telephones. They would produce evidence.

Nick listened with horrified fascination as first Whitney, then Whitney's wife, began calling up people. It became obvious that these people had trained themselves for just such an improbable caper by listening in on wiretaps. Whitney could imitate Roy's voice, and his wife could produce a passable version of Elsie's English accent. They would say things like, "This is Elsie, come on over, we're having a party. Bring some Scotch." Or Whitney, the bogus Commander, would call somebody and say, "We need a case of Glenlivet."

Elsie kept yelling, "I want to make a phone call, I want to call headquarters!" As they sat side by side on the sofa, Nick could feel Elsie next to him, vibrating with rage. Suddenly she got up and made a dive for the living room window. "My God," Nick thought, "she's going out that window and one of these apes is going to blow her apart with a shotgun!" Nick made a dive for Elsie, clasped her around the waist and pulled her back. He could see another agent, armed with a shotgun, waiting outside the window.

The phony calls went on. Some, who knew that Roy and Elsie would never have a liquor party in their home, were not fooled. But others began arriving with bottles and cases of the stuff. They were put under shotgun surveillance and herded into the Olmstead living room. One of the agents took a wooden case of liquor and plunked it down on the Italian-made dining table, gouging its polished surface and sending Elsie into another orbit of hysterical rage. As more people arrived there were more arrests and the place was filled with "evidence" in gunnysacks and boxes. Nick was surprised that even the gardener showed up with a couple of bottles in a wet gunnysack, and remembered thinking, "He had an aura about him that would drop a wet goat at 50 paces."

This bizarre business went on most of the night. Even Roy Lyle, the pacifier of the Anti-Saloon League, was making calls, pretending he was Olmstead, inviting people to bring booze to this big blast they were having at 3757 Ridgeway Place. The ludicrous scene took on another dimension when Elsie, who had been calm for a while, suddenly fell to the floor in convulsions of laughter. What set her off was one of Mrs. Whitney's phone calls to an Olmstead bootlegger, inviting him over in her practiced rendition of Elsie's accent. Elsie knew this fellow well, because he was German, and sometimes she would practice her own German on him over the phone. So, when Mrs. Whitney, babbled on, the man became suspicious and began speaking German to her. Mrs. Whitney, wide-eyed and baffled, held the telephone out away from her.

The decibel level gradually diminished about midnight. Some fifteen people had been suckered in by the phone calls and were arrested. Newspapers had been alerted by the agents, probably by Lyle, and reporters and cameramen were outside on the lawn. Camera flashbulbs went off as people moved ahead of shotguns and into police cars. Nick found himself in the back seat of a car driven by no less a personage than William M. Whitney himself.

Nick, feeling very much in need of a shot of evidence, sat in the middle, next to The Commander on his left. Roy was very quiet, Nick thought later, "like a lamb being led to the slaughter." On Nick's right was the gardener, smelling like a stable, and on her knees, leaning over the back of the front seat, was Mrs. Whitney. She was alternately giggling, raving, and sometimes shrieking, "We got'em! We got'em, goody, goody, goody!" None of this bothered Nick, even the smell of the gardener. What bothered him was the .45 automatic that Mrs. Whitney had pointed at them. Any second, Nick expected an explosion, because this nearly deranged woman had the hammer laid back on the .45 and obviously knew nothing about handguns. She waved the pistol loosely in front of Nick, Roy and the gardener, making her giggling, joyous noises on the way down to the police station.

Everybody was booked and put into cells. All except Nick. During the stormy hours at the Olmstead home, Nick had managed to go upstairs and retrieve his radio operator's license off the wall. When Nick produced his license, they didn't even book him, they just let him go. He was back on the street. The agent who escorted him out said, "Now you, junior, stay where you are, don't go out of town. We need you."

A free man, Nick walked in the rain back to his sleeping room. He would have many troubled times later, but at this moment, at least, he was away from that crazy woman with the gun. As he sat on the edge of his bed, Nick wondered what would become of Roy and Elsie, two people he had come to love. He thought of Roy's erect bearing, his unflappable confidence, his warmth and good humor. He never would forget Elsie's energy and generosity, her elegant ways, her laughter; and he would miss Aunt Vivian very much.

2

The Trial

In the winter weeks after that awful night in the Mount Baker house, Nick Foster did not leave Seattle, although he thought of making a run for it, perhaps to Canada, because he was not, after all, under arrest. The idea of bolting became especially tempting when the federal indictment came down on January 19, 1925—charging Roy Olmstead, and 90 others who worked for him, with conspiring to violate the National Prohibition Act.

Roy, out on bail, went right back to bootlegging. He hired more people, tightened up his operation, and continued to give Seattle the best of bourbon, Scotch and good gin. Roy was confident that he could not be convicted on wiretap evidence. He considered the raid on his Mount Baker home a farce.

Nothing had really changed, except that Seattle's children no longer heard about the adventures of "Bre'r Rabbit" and "Jackie Dumpling" on KFQX because the city's strongest radio station was now silent. Aunt Vivian had not been indicted, but she didn't try to operate the expensive, heavily draped, soundproof studio she had installed on the 21st floor of the Smith Tower.

Nick Foster's days were full of anxiety. He had not been arrested, to be sure, but he knew a lot about the Olmstead liquor empire. He had met some of Olmstead's gang of bootleggers, had watched illegal liquor money being counted and even knew where great amounts of cash were kept on Beacon Hill. This is what gnawed at him. He would be a splendid government witness. He had played the innocent when the federal agents came to his sleeping room and tried to pump him for information, but to be called up on a witness stand under oath, with the prosecutor tearing things out of him, would be awful. Nick thought he would be no good at perjury.

His testimony could damage Roy and Elsie. No matter that they were lawbreakers, Nick thought of them as the best people he had ever met.

Nick carried these thoughts around for almost a year, and when the trial of Roy Olmstead began on January 26, 1926, he stayed away from Judge Jeremiah Neterer's courtroom. He did not want to be seen because his very presence might trigger the idea of calling him to the stand. But Nick read the papers—the *Star*, the *Times*, the *Post-Intelligencer*, even the *Union Record*—and he followed the trial carefully.

Not all of the 90 defendants were there. Some of them had taken off for Canada: some had turned themselves in to Roy Lyle and William Whitney, the federal agents, offering to be witnesses in exchange for leniency. One of Roy's most trusted lieutenants, Al Hubbard, who had built Elsie's radio station, who had been with Olmstead on the night of the raid, became a turncoat. He bargained for, and got, a job as a federal prohibition agent, because he knew Olmstead's operation intimately and was wise in the ways of smuggling and bribery.

Even the Olmstead gang's attorney, Jerry Finch, had become obsolete. Finch himself was indicted. It was now down to the crunch, and Olmstead and 15 of his associates needed the best lawyer they could get. So, they trekked down to the Collins Building and hired George Vanderveer to defend them. There was nobody better.

George Vanderveer knew all about Roy Olmstead, and because he himself liked to toss back good whiskey he was like a lot of Seattle's citizens who felt indebted to Roy. Vanderveer knew a lot of Olmstead's gang members personally. As a young man, Vanderveer had hung out in Seattle's Skid Road district, and seaminess was no stranger to him; in fact, he was drawn to it. He knew by first name many of the seaport city's criminals, strikebreakers, con men, pimps and madams. He knew them well because he had defended them in his criminal law practice. Before that, he had served as assistant prosecuting attorney for King County. As prosecutor he had a spectacular—some said ruthless—conviction record.

In his earlier years, when he was young and more supple,

Vanderveer would go down to Skid Road and pick fights. He tangled with brewery-truck drivers, hard-drinking seamen and loggers, or he would taunt a soapbox orator into going at it on the sidewalk. He had a combative streak in him. He stood about 5 feet 9 inches tall, weighing about 165 pounds, but because he once had been on the boxing team at Stanford, he fancied himself a kind of Gentleman Jim Corbett, the clever boxing titlist at the turn of the century. Vanderveer could duke it out all right, and he was not afraid of bigger men. His slightly crooked nose was a souvenir of his street brawls.

Few of his clients had clean fingernails. Years later, two of Vanderveer's contemporaries, Ralph Potts and Lowell Hawley, would write a book about Vanderveer, which they called *Counsel for the Damned.*

Vanderveer had defended the IWW—the Wobblies—in the Centralia killing and the Everett massacre cases and had taken up the cause of labor's untouchables in Chicago and Detroit. Later, he represented the International Brotherhood of Teamsters during the labor violence on Seattle's streets and docks in the 1930s. Dave Beck, the head of the Teamsters, called Vanderveer "a better labor lawyer than Clarence Darrow," and some of Vanderveer's colleagues, who did not always admire his combative, even cynical, courtroom tactics, still placed him among the best criminal attorneys in the land.

So here came the Olmstead troops—the boatmen, the jiggermen, the truck drivers, the radio operators, the bookkeepers, checkers, transfer men—those who had worked under the Commander's discipline. And the Commander himself sat at Vanderveer's defense table.

From the beginning Judge Neterer's courtroom was crowded; the trial was front-page stuff, and if it did not turn into a circus, it soon became a very good show.

The city was divided over Roy's trial. There were the clubwomen, the anti-saloon forces, and the clergy—very much the clergy—led by that gangling, oratorical enemy of sin, the Rev. Mark Matthews, whose righteous fortress, the First Presbyterian Church, housed 9,000 members. The Rev. Matthews, a powerful force in the community, had hardened moral convictions. He was given to extremism. According to historian Norman Clark, he held that the law was sovereign and eternal and "ought to be enforced if every street in America had to run with blood and every cobblestone had to be made of a human skull."

Roy Olmstead used to tease the Rev. Matthews. When he met the reverend on the street he would greet him cheerily and advise him not to take life too seriously. Roy would even inquire after the quality of his parishioners' medicinal brandy, which Roy had bootlegged into Seattle.

In the beginning, George Vanderveer thought of his case as another bootlegging caper. The public expected an easy conviction. One of Roy's boats, the Eva B., had been seized with 784 cases of liquor and three defendants aboard. Though they found no liquor the night of the raid on Olmstead's Mount Baker home, the agents had seized records of his organization. There were the defectors, too, including the knowledgeable and treacherous Al Hubbard.

Nick Foster, it appeared, had no cause to worry about being called. The case against Olmstead seemed tight enough.

But soon Vanderveer perceived that he was into something far more significant than bootlegging; he was into an issue of profound national importance, one that involved the Fourth and Fifth Amendments to the U.S. Constitution. Much of the prosecution's case, as represented by U.S. District Attorney Thomas P. Revelle, rested on the telephone taps made on Olmstead's Mount Baker home. Nick Foster had warned Roy about those taps, but Olmstead, secure in the belief that such taps were inadmissible as evidence—hell, wiretapping was itself illegal— refused to worry about them.

But early in the trial, Judge Neterer began admitting the taps. Vanderveer turned furious. "There is a statute in the state of Washington that forbids wiretapping; it is against the law," he argued. To make matters worse, outraging Vanderveer even more, the taps themselves were suspect. They were rough, penciled notes made by Whitney's emotionally charged wife. She then typed up pages off the notes to be used in court. She had destroyed the original notes. During the trial, her transcripts became known as "the book."

Vanderveer went on the offensive. Ralph Potts later would write: "By the time he was well into the case, there can be little doubt that he had convinced himself that the basic liberties of Americans yet unborn rested squarely upon his shoulders."

Vanderveer argued that it was unthinkable, even obscene, to use unlawfully obtained material as a way to enforce the law. The typed notes were used to refresh the memories of government witnesses. Vanderveer objected; he was overruled by Judge Neterer, who would not allow the defense to examine "the book." As the trial went on, Vanderveer kept hammering at the question of admissibility. A star government witness was the wealthy maker of airplanes, William E. Boeing, who testified that, yes, Olmstead had supplied him with liquor. The best of liquor, to be sure.

Potts noted that Vanderveer's technique "was not unlike that of a legal toreador, taunting and tormenting" the patient Judge Neterer. He skirted the edge of contempt with his sarcasm, never more closely than when he said to the court, "I want a fair, decent white man's chance to test the truth of this, that is all."

Neterer shot back: "Just a minute. When you address the court employ language that is fitting for the occasion."

"I am," said Vanderveer.

The case against Olmstead began to attract national attention. Eastern papers called it the "whispering wires" case. Legal scholars began to show up in Judge Neterer's court. Law students came from the University of Washington.

Olmstead seemed to enjoy the trial immensely; he had a taste for irony, as Norman Clark put it, "Olmstead roared with laughter as some of the phony telephone calls, the product of his own humor, were brought in evidence against him." He was more amused than angered by the testimony of William E. Boeing. Roy even had supplied one of the assistant prosecutors with good, unadulterated Canadian booze. What more can a man do to quench a civic thirst?

The trial went on for weeks, splashed along in the newspapers, and many Seattle citizens hoped it would never end. But it did have to end sometime. Roy Olmstead was found guilty. On March 29, 1926, Judge Neterer sentenced him to four years at hard labor in a federal prison. Roy was fined $8,000. Twenty-three other defendants were convicted and sentenced. Jerry Finch, the Olmstead gang's attorney, was one of them.

The great cloud of guilt and fear was lifted from Nick Foster's daily life. He had not been called to testify, and he was pleased that

Elsie Olmstead went free. Of course, there was no more Aunt Vivian because the Olmsteads were broke. The easy-come money was gone. It went into paying off employees and into attorney's fees; a lot of it had gone earlier into the pockets of Seattle's finest.

Roy went free on bail, but to raise money, he and Elsie sold their lovely home on Ridgeway Place. They had to sell the imported furniture too, and their radio station, KFQX.

Ultimately, KFQX was taken over by the Fisher family and its call letters were changed to KOMO. KOMO became one of Seattle's most powerful and respected radio stations.

With Roy gone, the downtown boys, knocking them back in their private clubs and speakeasies, had to pay much more for good whiskey. Sometimes they couldn't even buy the stuff.

Vanderveer appealed. He argued before the Circuit Court of Appeals in San Francisco that use of wiretap evidence violated the search-and-seizure clause of the Fourth Amendment. It was no longer a booze runner's trial. The case of the United States v. Olmstead took on a profound meaning for every citizen of the United States.

Vanderveer lost the appeal. The majority of judges saw no need to reverse Judge Neterer, but one man, a lone dissenter, made the difference. Circuit Judge Frank H. Rudkin had no doubt that the bootleggers, including Olmstead, were guilty. But he did not like the use of Mrs. Whitney's typed "book" as evidence; he did not like the manner in which the trial was conducted. The book, and not the witnesses, was the important flaw. "A better opportunity to color or fabricate testimony could not be devised by the wit of man," he wrote.

Judge Rudkin's dissent paved the way for a petition to the U.S. Supreme Court. As Norman Clark would write, "Wiretapping was a new problem in official morality, a murky and treacherous one in no way illuminated by federal legislation." Vanderveer sent his friend, John F. Dore, later to be a two-term mayor of Seattle, to argue the petition for review. The Supreme Court eventually agreed to hear one issue: "whether the use of evidence of private telephone conversations … intercepted by means of wiretapping is in violation of the Fourth and Fifth Amendments …"

With Olmstead out on bail once more, the case was heard in February 1928. The Supreme Court affirmed the conviction. Chief

Justice William Howard Taft wrote the majority opinion, saying in part that "a standard which would forbid the reception of evidence if obtained by other than nice ethical conduct by government officials would make society suffer and give criminals greater immunity than has been known heretofore."

Four justices dissented: Pierce Butler, Harlan Stone, Louis Brandeis and Oliver Wendell Holmes. Justice Brandeis wrote a dissent that would, less than a year later, send Congress scurrying to pass a law forbidding use of wiretaps, a dissent that has become a classic statement of Americans' right to privacy.

"Discovery and invention," said Brandeis, "have made it possible for the government, by means far more effective than stretching upon a rack, to obtain disclosure in court what is whispered in the closet .... as a means of espionage, writs of assistance and general warrants are but puny instruments of tyranny and oppression when compared with wiretapping ...."

Brandeis told how the makers of the Constitution "undertook to secure conditions favorable to the pursuit of happiness .... they conferred, as against the government, the right to be left alone-the most comprehensive of rights and the right most valued by civilized men ...."

As for Whitney and his agents who relied on illegal wiretaps, Justice Brandeis concluded with words that have been quoted many times since: "In a government of laws, existence of government will be imperiled if it fails to observe the laws scrupulously .... if the government becomes a lawbreaker, it breeds contempt for the law ....it invites anarchy .... Against that pernicious doctrine this court should resolutely set its face."

That was the ball game.

Though he lost Olmstead's appeal to the Supreme Court, George Vanderveer had won his crusade. This may have been small comfort to Olmstead's gang, serving their time at McNeil Island, or to Olmstead himself, although he would say at the time, "I'm not complaining, I broke the law."

Olmstead served his full sentence at McNeil. He spent much time in the prison library. He turned into an omnivorous reader, particularly on religion. He became a disciple of Mary Baker Eddy.

After his release, Roy spent the rest of his life as a Christian Science practitioner, operating out of an office he rented in the White-Henry-Stuart Building. He frequently gave lectures on the evils of drink. Many years later, when historian Norman Clark interviewed Olmstead, the ex-bootlegger told him, "The old Roy Olmstead is dead. He no longer exists."

All of them are gone now-the charming Elsie and her Aunt Vivian; Al Hubbard, the clever informer; the odoriferous gardener; Mr. Dapper, the bagman with the Stutz Bearcat; the cops who delivered liquor from their sidecars; Vanderveer and John Dore, Judge Neterer, William Whitney, Roy Lyle; all the lawyers, all the justices, all those who gave and took bribes. With the possible exception of a few rugged survivors, all of them are gone, the men and women of Seattle's roaring '20s who drank the very best of liquor because they had Roy Olmstead-the honest bootlegger.

Nick Foster lived a long and happy life.

Following the trial, Nick went to work for the General Electric Company, where he stayed for 14 years. He then became a teacher in the Seattle school system, where he worked until his retirement in 1971. Nick taught radio engineering for many years at Edison Vocational School, and during this time, shortly after World War II, he met Dorothy Bullitt, who owned a small station, KEVR, located in the Smith Tower. Dorothy Bullitt would later change her station's call letters to KING.

Mrs. Bullitt and Nick became good friends.

They would meet over coffee on occasion, and one day, after television began coming in, Nick told her he knew she had an extra FM transmitter. He said the city school district and its Edison Vocational School would like to have a transmitter. He told Dorothy, "I wouldn't want to insult you by offering what we can afford to pay for it, so I don't see that there is any way out except that you give it to us."

Dorothy Bullitt, who was not given to easy smiles, smiled then. In three days Edison Vocational owned a 10,000-watt FM transmitter; with it came an eight-bay, cloverleaf-type antenna. Nick figured the transmitter was worth, perhaps, forty-five thousand dollars and the antenna about eight thousand.

As it happened, Dorothy Bullitt's KING television station went on the air in 1948. By 1952, it became apparent that KING needed a more powerful TV transmitter, a fact that overjoyed Nick Foster up at Edison Vocational. This meant that KING-TV would have a spare transmitter. As Nick put it later, "My avarice is going up and I start working again-pleading and button holing everybody I can." One day Nick got a call from KING-TV's director of engineering, James Middlebrook, a man he had buttonholed.

"If you repeat this," said Middlebrook, "I will deny it, but you are the new owner of a TG5A television transmitter—complete. So, you are going to have to think about coming and getting it. My God," he added, "don't say anything for another week."

As Nick also knew, Dorothy Bullitt did not advertise her generosity.

The transmitter from Channel 5 had to be rebuilt to accommodate what Nick was shooting for—Seattle's first educational TV outlet, Channel 9. Nick went to Los Angeles to a National Association of Broadcasters convention and brought back a pile of technical literature on the transmitter he had just inherited. He gave the literature to his Edison Vocational students, and within days they knew every facet of the transmitter.

As Nick recalled it later, "We sort of moved around like a queen bee and a bunch of swarming bees, but with our own tools, and some specialized parts we scrounged, we converted Dorothy Bullitt's old transmitter from one frequency to another—Channel 5 into Channel 9."

Running low on money, Nick located a smashed-up antenna in Salt Lake City and bought it for $600. Over many weeks of intricate, painstaking work, Nick and his students rebuilt the tower, girder by girder, cable by cable.

It was a near miracle. Nick and his 15 Edison Vocational students put together a full, working TV station, complete with antenna.

"Everybody kind of decided," Nick recalled later, that since we didn't have any studio, we didn't have any facilities, our rig should be on the University of Washington campus. Let them make the application for the license. In other words, me, and my group of 15 job-training students, put up this rig and maintained it for thirteen years. Thirteen years we had that rig on the air and it never cost the school district or anyone a dime-except for the power it took to run it.

"So, KCTS became a transmitting entity and was maintained and operated by us, me and my students, until such time as the UW got the money for a new transmitter and anew antenna, which has been on 18th and Madison to this day. That first studio was manned, not entirely, but in large part, by class members of Edison Vocational School.

"I retired from teaching in 1971. Now and then I think back on Roy and Aunt Vivian. I never saw them again. Elsie and Roy, they were two of the finest people I ever knew. I think of them both a lot ... and Roy and all those wild days. I think life was kind of a sweet dream to him."

In 1935, Roy Olmstead was granted a full pardon by President Franklin D. Roosevelt

3

Big Bertha

I might have been eight years old when my father, at the supper table, exploded with a splendid name that caught even my young ear. The name was "Big Bertha." I would learn later that Big Bertha originally was the nickname of a 209.8-millimeter cannon the Germans used in World War I to shell Paris from 75 miles away. "Big Bertha" had an awesome sound to it, and here is the way my father used it at our supper table in West Seattle.

He had finished reading the evening *Seattle Star*, which was then regarded as a working man's paper (he hated Hearst and the *Post-Intelligencer* and had no use for the *Times*), and he had read something about City Light, some kind of public scrimmage that involved the head of City Light, J.D. Ross, and private power interests.

"By God, they'd better be careful now," he exulted, referring to the private power people. "They'll have more'n they can handle if they get Big Bertha after them."

My father, like many working people in Seattle, did not trust private power or the people who profited from it. Like most Seattleites then, he was rock solid in his support of public power. So, he was pleased to read that Mr. Ross, who had become a public issue as director of City Light, had the firm backing of Seattle's mayor.

Big Bertha.

It was a name used in admiring jest that implied integrity and power. It was also used derisively by many a malefactor, bootlegger, dance hall operator, gambler or crooked cop, of which Seattle had an abundant supply.

The lady was, of course, Bertha Knight Landes, Seattle's first and only woman mayor. For one brief shining moment, Bertha K. Landes became an authentic national heroine.

She fascinated, then captivated, the national press. In 1926 Bertha K. Landes became the first woman to be elected mayor of any large American city.

Who was this woman who could make a quiet man like my father explode with joy, who could shut down whorehouses, shake a police department to its corrupt underpinnings, stop wide-open gambling, and treat chiefs of police and other satraps as adolescent miscreants? Because of the lady they called "Big Bertha," this city of 250,000, tucked off in a remote corner of the Northwest, would stand, however briefly, in the national spotlight. She was a phenomenon, decades ahead of her time, who inspired her admirers and enraged her enemies, the machos of the '20s who thought "petticoat government" was an embarrassment no city could bear.

Bertha was, in many ways, the quintessential Seattle woman, the kind of woman who devoted herself to good works; was adept at cooking, sewing, knitting and seeing to the comfort of her husband. The wife of a geology professor at the University of Washington, Mayor Landes was often pictured in an apron, serving dinner to her husband.

She lived in an age when women were unabashedly referred to as "the weaker sex" and men routinely referred to their wives as "the little woman."

Bertha K. Landes was not little, really. She was on the stoutish side and just looked small when standing next to a burly chief of police. In 1926 the *New York Times* described her as "below medium height, with olive skin and drab brown hair." The good gray *Times* did not mention her roundish figure but remarked on "the keen brightness of her eyes" as being "her most arresting feature."

She wore those hats—the proper, severe, tight-fitting hats in the style of the time—and while the skirts of 1920s Seattle women inched daringly higher, as they did everywhere else, those of Bertha Knight Landes stayed low to the floor. In appearance and dress, she was reminiscent of the old tintypes of great-grandmothers in millions of family albums. Mrs. Landes looked like the stem proprietress of a respectable boarding house.

She served for only two years as mayor, 1926 to 1928, and because

Seattle has had colorful mayors like Hy Gill, Ole Hanson, Honest Tom Hume and Johnny Dore, Mrs. Landes has received little attention from historians. Only few today know about "Big Bertha."

One exception is Doris Pieroth, a Seattle writer and historian. "She brought to the role of public servant," Pieroth has written, "fifty-three years of previous experience as daughter, sister, student, wife, pioneer, mother, community leader and clubwoman."

Clubwoman indeed. At one time or another, Bertha K. Landes belonged to almost every club in town. She even founded some of them. A charter member of the Minutewomen of Washington, she organized various Red Cross auxiliaries in World War I. She was national president of the Soroptimist Clubs. She became a leader in the Woman's Century Club and the Women's University Club. She served as president of the Seattle League of Women Voters and the Seattle Federation of Women's Clubs, and as moderator of the Congregational Church Conference of Washington.

The woman mayor's adopted daughter, Mrs. E. J. Peach, told an interviewer years ago: "She wasn't aggressive, but if she wasn't engaged in planning something or other, she was bored to tears." Mrs. Peach noted that her mother was "the grandest woman you could know" and "there was no one kindlier or more tolerant."

Friends urged Bertha Landes to run for the City Council in 1922. She won by a record-breaking plurality of 22,000 votes. Mrs. Landes, along with a woman aptly named Katherine Miracle, who also was elected to the council, had broken the all-male hold on Seattle politics.

During her first term on the council, Mrs. Landes fought for tighter controls on Seattle's cabarets and dance halls and emerged as a powerful and intelligent proponent of public power. But the resounding boom of Big Bertha was yet to be heard.

The cannon was loaded in 1924 when Bertha Landes was elected president of the City Council. Until then Seattle was a wide-open, anything-goes seaport presided over by a mayor named Edwin J. (Doc) Brown, a confidant of bootleggers, gamblers and cops. Doc advertised himself as a "painless" dentist. He was a friend and convivial buddy of Roy Olmstead, king of Northwest bootleggers. The police chief, William Severyns, ran his department with a loose and tolerant hand.

Doc Brown decided to attend the Democratic National Convention in Philadelphia that year and looked forward to turning his trip into a month-long getaway from the rigors of office. As council president, Mrs. Landes would be the city's acting mayor while Doc was off having fun. When Doc Brown installed Mrs. Landes as caretaker of his office, at an informal meeting that included Chief Severyns, the transition was jovial enough.

"There isn't much to do here," he said, then added with smile, "but keep your eye on the chief."

Bertha Landes had had her eye on the chief for quite a while and was not amused by what she saw. She knew in a general way about the bootlegging, Skid Road whorehouses, dice games, blackjack and poker games, all in full view of anyone who cared to see. Like many another citizen she had taken note of an unguarded remark by Chief Severyns, which appeared in a Seattle newspaper. What the chief had let slip was that a hundred Seattle policemen should not be on the force. A casual remark, but the implications were plain enough-that many Seattle cops were on the take.

So, Bertha K. Landes, sitting in as mayor, summoned Chief Severyns to her office. She said, "You will fire one hundred policemen, or you will resign yourself."

The chief resisted. A testy exchange of letters followed. Mrs. Landes wrote to Severyns: "Now if a statement made by you that there are 100 men on the police force who should not be there is true, then it must follow as a logical conclusion that 100 men should be removed .... I desire immediate results and a written statement, within 24 hours, from you acknowledging the receipt of my order."

The chief replied with a letter of his own, about 1,200 typed words of patronizing, bureaucratic flatulence.

In one windy passage, Severyns said he was unafraid and undisturbed, "according to the light that leadeth every man that cometh into the world."

Confident that he could face down the housewife and clubwoman, Severyns pointed out that the city charter allowed the mayor to take over the police department in a time of crisis.

He added with condescending sarcasm: "You should find solace and consolation in that wholesome provision."

With that, it was good-bye, Chiefie.

Bertha K. Landes fired him on the spot. She also fired the assistant chief, Joe Mason, who was so mixed up in the Severyns' system that he begged off trying to carry out her demand for reforms.

The next day the headlines blared:

"Landes Appoints Herself Chief!"

Within hours, every gambling joint and speakeasy in Seattle was locked up tight. Slot machines were turned to the wall. Bootleg liquor deliveries slowed. Chinese lotteries were stopped. Seattle was a buttoned-down city.

Oh, there were some grins, all right. So, the slots couldn't run, and you couldn't roll a hard eight. Just wait'll Doc Brown gets back.

Doc Brown, trying to relax in the distant East, found himself deluged with frantic telegrams. "Get back here right now," they said in effect, "and stop this one-woman reform squad."

It took several days for Mayor Brown to get back to Seattle from Philadelphia. By then, Mrs. Landes was serving simultaneously as mayor, chief of police, and president of the City Council. No public official in the city's history had ever held such power.

Doc returned, finally. He put Severyns back in as chief. The gambling joints opened again, the speakeasies went full blast once more, and the cops resumed taking their payoffs. Things were back to normal. Seattle was an "action city" again, and all was well, "according to the light that leadeth every man that cometh into the world."

But wait a minute, what was that sound out there? Does a political ground swell have a sound, does it make a noise that you can hear, or do you just feel it? But if it sounds like a sound, what IS that sound? Why, it was a city in a restless mood, a city taking stock of itself, a city that no longer wanted to be in thrall to a bunch of hogs wallowing in the public trough. No, by God, there's more to this city than a cluster of easily accessible cathouses and corrupt hooligans and card rooms.

They wanted her to run for mayor. They wanted this direct, courageous lady to send Honest Doc, the painless dentist, back to his vials of Novocain.

The clubwomen especially wanted one of their own in the mayor's chair. But a sizeable number of men, too, disgusted with Seattle under Doc Brown, felt it was time to give this woman a chance. Quite a few businessmen had gotten to know Bertha Landes as level-headed, conservative and, above all, committed to living in a decent city.

Mrs. Landes was reluctant to run for mayor. She liked being a housewife. She liked cooking at home, mothering the students at the university, feeding them baked beans and com bread in the evenings. Her husband, Henry Landes, was a distinguished scientist and head of the geology department. He had served an interim term in 1914-15 as president of the university.

For a long time, the Landeses lived in a big house, with an inviting front porch, where the Meany Tower Hotel now stands. Later, because Bertha spent so much more time on civic affairs, the Landeses moved to the Wilsonian Apartments on University Way. Now, with this mayor business ... for one of the few times in her life, Bertha Landes was unsure of what she wanted.

Pressure on her to run came from everywhere. Working class citizens, thousands of neighborhood people, and all three of Seattle's daily papers urged her to wade in and get a little mud on her shoes. She changed her mind several times and finally agreed to run only two hours before filing deadline.

Mrs. Landes got a high rating from the Municipal League. She said she would campaign for a ballot initiative to establish a city management form of government in Seattle-a measure which, if it were passed and she were elected, would end her job as mayor. She said she would campaign for public power, for a better street railway system, and for strongly enforced traffic safety measures.

She meant to be a strong mayor. "I will attend to other duties than greeting actresses at incoming trains," she said.

A city was nothing more than a larger family, Mrs. Landes argued, and "home standards should be city standards."

She stuck with her view that a woman's first duty was to her husband and to her family. And Henry Landes, the geology professor, said he found nothing "revolutionary" in his wife's candidacy.

"It's simply the natural enlargement of her sphere," he told the *New York Times*. "Keeping house and raising a family are woman's logical tasks, and, in principle, there's no difference between running one home and a hundred thousand."

Doris Pieroth points out that Mrs. Landes' campaign for mayor "occurred against the backdrop of the celebrated 'Rum Trial' of

Seattle." The trial of cop turned bootlegger Roy Olmstead and many of his cohorts was played out on the front pages-a trial that "tended to substantiate links between Brown and bootleg interests and to corroborate assertions she had made during the Severyns firing in 1924."

Old Doc Brown never had a chance. And so, it was that on March 9, 1926, in a record voter turnout, Seattle's first woman mayor was elected by 6,000 votes. She was 57 at the time.

Because she was the first woman to be mayor of any large city in America, the Eastern press was fascinated by Mrs. Landes. A roving correspondent from the *Brooklyn Eagle* dropped into town to see how she handled the chronic squabbling among law enforcement agencies that had hamstrung law enforcement as much as corruption had.

"Forty-eight hours after she had been inaugurated," he wrote, "Mayor Landes called a meeting of the Chief of Police, the Sheriff, the Prohibition Enforcement Director, the Captain of the Coast Guard, the heads of the local Secret Service bureau and representatives of the Department of Justice. These lions all came to her office and departed, some three hours later, transformed into lambs."

As mayor she was outstanding. She pushed to establish a public hospital and embarked on a campaign to cut down on traffic accidents, of which she said, "Lives are sacrificed to carelessness, love of speed and love of that which befogs the mind and deadens muscular control." Police Court receipts went up by 50 percent.

She owed no special interest, and she had no agenda beyond being the best mayor Seattle ever had.

Each morning an official chauffeur picked up Mayor Landes at the Wilsonian Apartments on University Way. She arrived at City Hall no later than 9 a.m. She put in long hours and, on most evenings, gave speeches, her own, written in longhand. In her speeches, she exhorted Seattle women to become aware, to become involved in community doings, to look up from their dishpans and see the wider world in a great city.

If you don't get involved in public affairs, she told high school students, "you are simply saying that you are unfit to live in a free community."

Pieroth cites another speech Mrs. Landes made shortly after being sworn in as mayor: "The city," she said, "is really only a larger household or family with its problems increased many fold through its diversified interests and the cosmopolitan nature of its members."

This went down well with the clubwomen and even brought approving nods from professional people and those businessmen who were not immersed in the Babbitry of total self-interest.

But it didn't go over with the cops. Or the firemen, either. It didn't ring any bells with them because one of Mrs. Landes' crusades was that of tightening up the Civil Service Commission.

She was one busy lady. She revamped the Board of Public Works and when it came to political appointments, she proved to be a mayor of monumental ingratitude. Instead of appointing political supporters-the old spoils system-she called upon qualified professionals to guide the city's technical departments. She waded into the thicket of Seattle's finances, instituted improvements in City Light and the street railway system. She helped found the City Planning Commission (a body that still functions today) and was far ahead of her time in pushing for a merger of county and city governments.

She impressed the daily newspapers. *The Seattle Times* wrote, "Those who call upon her come on business and not to sit around and smoke, gossip and plot for the confusion of a rival faction."

And always there were those speeches. "Play the game fairly," she exhorted. "Meet life honestly—never whine and play the coward but take life as it comes …. Don't be a shirker but do be a worker. Above all, so conduct yourself that you can look your own soul in the face. You cannot be true to yourself without being true to everyone else."

The boys on the curb didn't like such high-sounding talk. The town was not closed down absolutely tight. Mrs. Landes was a realist, and she was not, as Pieroth points out, an unwavering bluenose. But the men would gather up at Doc Hamilton's place, boozing it up a little and shooting craps, and they would call her "Big Bertha," as though it was an epithet.

The talk went on in downtown eating places like Rippe's and Manca's and probably, to some extent, in the Rainier Club, that bastion of total male-ism where women were admitted, if at all, through a side entrance.

To get her out of office, the anti-Landes forces picked a political nonentity, a former movie-theater proprietor named Frank Edwards. He was one of those bland airheads that entrenched interests always seem to choose when they want to keep things going exactly as they like it.

Edwards became mysteriously endowed with bountiful campaign funds. He began his run for mayor while Mrs. Landes was working on tough problems during her second year in office. Edwards had no visible qualifications to replace her; he had no record of any public service and had not, as far as anyone could tell, ever become involved in community affairs.

Edwards' campaign was long and costly. He began his run to unseat Mrs. Landes fully nine months before the election of 1928. The Municipal League, examining this White Knight of the male establishment, found Edwards "sadly lacking" in qualifications, while pronouncing Mrs. Landes a "very capable and dignified mayor."

The big money against her came from private power interests, "open town" advocates, cops and firemen, and males too discomfited by "petticoat government."

From the beginning, the campaign centered on whether Mrs. Landes, or any woman, should be in charge of a city. The red-noses wanted her out of there. Edwards was said to have more than 50 scandalmongers on his payroll.

The issue was always about having a woman in office, nothing truly nasty, but always the "woman issue," the jokes, the wisecracks, the taunts. Seattle did not like being teased about "petticoat politics," and its men burned under the sarcasm from other cities: "What's the matter with you folks out there? Haven't you got any men available-you need a woman for mayor?"

Edwards, smart enough to be wary, avoided any contact with this lady of superior intellectual firepower. Mrs. Landes may have been the first American political candidate to debate an empty chair. She would set up mock contests with Edwards, the absentee candidate, and the New York Times reported that "she laughs as she conducts these one-sided debates and appears to get as much 'kick' out of them as her hearers, and the audience is usually in an uproar."

In the end, of course, they beat her-with money, and what we now call male chauvinism. Though she won in the primary, Mrs. Landes went down under an avalanche in the final, 58,033 for Edwards, 39,889 for Mrs. Landes. She was a one-term mayor.

Edwards, the nonentity, would later be recalled by irate Seattle voters after he fired the popular J. D. Ross as head of City Light.

Julia M. Budlong, a writer for *The Nation*, asked a pointed question: "Was the burden of living under a New England conscience too great for the frontier village?" The press postmortems all pointed directly to the fact that Mrs. Landes was a woman. The Portland *Oregonian*, having reviewed Mrs. Landes' undoubted skills and Edwards' lack of them, said, "We suspect, in the light of these facts, that Mrs. Landes was defeated solely because Seattle wishes to be known as a he-man's town." It went on to suggest that a pair of breeches be hung from the flagpole at City Hall.

To the everlasting relief of Seattle's he-men, "Big Bertha" was finished. She never held public office again. *The Nation*, in a summing up, said that Seattle "is a little ashamed of itself" for having turned her out, and ventured that, if the election were to be held again, she would be voted back in. "Seattle begins to remember," it said, "what an awfully good mayor Mrs. Landes was."

As a private citizen she remained extraordinarily active in Seattle's public life. In 1931, during the Great Depression, Mayor Robert Harlin appointed her chairman of the Women's Employment Committee-a subdivision of the city's Unemployment Commission. She rallied the city's business leaders and set up an employment clearing house for women who needed work. She soon had several thousand of them earning money by sewing.

She also took the lead in eliminating the "white only" restriction for membership in the Soroptimist Clubs. As Doris Pieroth has written: "That is a rational note for an era marked by agitation for immigrant exclusion and virulent racism-a time in which 50 hooded and robed members of the Ku Klux Klan could be seated in a body for Sunday services at Seattle's First Presbyterian Church and be described by the Rev. Mark Matthews as worshiping 'reverentially.' "

An excellent writer, she wrote several retrospective pieces on her life in politics for national publications, including *Collier's*. She traveled widely with her husband and spoke before many luncheon groups and conventions.

Henry Landes died in 1936, and by 1939 Mrs. Landes' own health was beginning to fail. She lived on at the Wilsonian. In 1941 she moved from Seattle to Pacific Palisades in California and on November 29, 1943, she died at her son's home in Ann Arbor, Michigan. She was 75.

"Play the game fairly," she had said. "Meet life honestly-never whine and play the coward but take life as it comes."

She did all of that and more. Big Bertha was a great lady, and Seattle became a better city because she was here.

In an eloquent passage, Doris Pieroth has written: "The attempt to meet political success took her beyond the stereotype of municipal housekeeper to meet politics on her own terms, and she found herself, a woman beyond the home, at odds with her culture if not with herself."

4

Little Boy Lost

It was June 3, 1935, and the old Civic Field, a pebble-strewn, bare-dirt, low-rent baseball park, was alive with hundreds of kids. There was no grass at all, in either the outfield or the infield. The field was surrounded by tin fences, which easily bent enough for us to sneak in and watch the old Seattle Indians play at night.

For all of its dusty hardness, Civic Field was sacred ground. On this repellent, skinned diamond there trod such hometown heroes as "Highpockets" Bill Lawrence, Dick Gyselman, Alan Strange, Levi "Chief" McCormick, Hal Spindel, Jerry Donovan, Mike Hunt, Dick Barrett and Hal Turpin. Seattle was in the Pacific Coast League, which included such distant cities as San Diego, San Francisco and Los Angeles. And on the hardpan surface we watched the likes of Joe DiMaggio, of San Francisco, take his first steps toward baseball's Hall of Fame.

The team was then owned by George Vanderveer, the great criminal-and-labor attorney who lived near Franklin High School. He was going broke trying to keep the minor league franchise afloat. He was so broke, he tried to give it away, free, to Dave Beck, the powerful head of the local Teamsters Union. Beck was a baseball fan, but he said, "No, George, no. I couldn't afford the first-baseman's salary." It was the bottom of the Great Depression.

There was a free "baseball school" in progress. We kids, showed up in sweat shirts and bent caps. Many of us wore Keds, not spiked baseball shoes, and some of us wore dark brown "commissary cords," free clothing from the federal government. But we were rich in dreams. We, too, would be the next DiMaggio.

There must have been a dozen instructors, mostly high school coaches and semi-pro managers, at this baseball school. Among them were Frank "Bush" Tobin, a catcher of Coast League caliber, and Bobby Morris, famed on weekends as a college football referee.

And there was "Tubby" Graves, who coached baseball at the University of Washington. Tubby was a big man, wide in the hips, big feet, with a way of slouching when he walked. He had a booming, friendly voice, full of laughter, and being from Missouri, he had a slightly southern accent and a poetic gift for memorable similes and imagery.

"Over here!" he boomed. "Over here by the fence, we're going to learn how to hit."

So maybe two dozen of us future DiMaggios stood around Tubby near the left-field fence and he was swinging a bat idly in his huge hands.

Then he said: "Let's imagine you have just cornered the Weyerhaeuser kidnapper. You're gonna hit the Weyerhaeuser kidnapper in the belly."

Tubby held his bat high over his shoulder, waving it in exaggerated circles above his head. "Too much motion, too much wasted time," he said. "You're never gonna hit the Weyerhaeuser kidnapper that way. He'll either be gone or he'll move in and take the bat away from you."

Tubby drew himself into a compact batting stance, the bat cocked and still. "There's his belly, now you swing. No waste motion, no fancy stuff, just—wham! Right into the Weyerhaeuser kidnapper's belly."

It was the perfect analogy. Every kid knew what Tubby Graves was talking about. The Weyerhaeuser kidnapping! It was all over—on radio, in newspapers, in restaurants, on street corners. This was the story that consumed the Northwest and the nation.

Outside, on our way to Civic Field that morning, were the headlines: "Family Fails to Contact Weyerhaeuser Kidnapper," "Hunt for Kidnappers Centers in Seattle-Death Threatened."

The Weyerhaeuser kidnapping occurred at 11:45 on Friday morning, May 24, 1935.

The boy was picked up and forced into the back seat of a car while on his way home to lunch from Lowell Grammar School in Tacoma. Little George Hunt Weyerhaeuser was nine years old. He was a fourth-generation Weyerhaeuser, scion of a family that owned great stands of timber in Washington, Oregon, Idaho, Arkansas, Vermont, Oklahoma and several other states.

Most of us couldn't spell the name of the enormously wealthy family who lived in Tacoma. The Weyerhaeusers were reserved and private. Yet now, suddenly, they were as well-known as Charles A. Lindbergh, the legendary flyer whose son had been kidnapped and coldly murdered two years before.

Police, sheriffs' deputies from three counties, criminologists and so-called kidnapping experts descended on Tacoma. J. Edgar Hoover, then the Mr. Clean director of the Federal Bureau of Investigation, sent teams of field agents to Tacoma.

More than 50 newspaper people almost overwhelmed the Weyerhaeuser home at 420 North Fourth Street, a two-story mansion overlooking Commencement Bay. There were lead stories and human-interest sidebars. One of the *Seattle Times* reporters was Paul O'Neil, who later wrote cover stories for *Time, Life* and *Sports Illustrated*. "Chin up, George! Don't let it get you down, boy," was the headline over one O'Neil story on the kidnapping. Nothing, it seemed, went uncovered. "George Manly Little Man, Says His Tacoma Barber." George's barber was Oliver DeBalt, whose chair was in the Winthrop Hotel, and he had granted an exclusive interview to the *Times*.

The *Times* appointed an anonymous "Kidnap Editor" to handle tips and information from readers.

Most newspapers said the kidnapping was the work of a disciplined mob rumored to be from the Midwest. The "Karpis Gang" got hefty play. So did U.S. Marshal A. J. Chitty, who pronounced the kidnapping "a big-league job." Luke S. May, of the Seattle Police Department, a celebrated clue-finder of the day, was into the case. Another prominent cop answered to the euphonious name of 0. K. Badia, 0. K. was widely quoted on theories and clues.

George Weyerhaeuser was a slender boy, 4 feet 5 ¼ inches tall, with curly brown hair and brown eyes. When he disappeared, George was wearing a sweater, brown corduroy pants and Keds tennis shoes. One acquaintance described George as "the manliest little man" he had ever known. His fifth-grade teacher, a Miss Berg at Lowell Grammar School, said George was "an alert obedient and brilliant pupil, having a smiling, handsome face, with no distinguishing marks."

On his way home to lunch that day in May the day of the kidnapping George practiced broad jumping (he wanted to be a track star). He skipped through the grounds of the Tacoma Lawn and Tennis Club, then climbed a flight of stairs up to the main street. A tan Buick was parked next to the curb. A man stood beside it. The man grabbed George, put his hand over his mouth, and threw him to the floor below the back seat of the car. He covered George with a blanket and told him not to yell or try to move. He put a blindfold on the boy.

The tan Buick then rolled down the hill out of the quiet residential neighborhood. It threaded its way along Tacoma streets and quickly was on rural back roads. When George's blindfold was removed, he was in the woods, the sound of a river nearby. He could see two men wearing hoods with eyeholes.

George was put into a pit dug in the woods. The pit was about three feet long and was covered with tin and braced with boards. One arm and one leg were handcuffed to a crosspiece in the bottom of the pit. He was told write his name on the back of an envelope and again on the back of the ransom note.

The ransom note was mailed, special delivery, the evening of the kidnapping. It was a long note to the family containing 21 points, the first five of which specified that the ransom was to be $200,000 in cash, to consist of $100,000 in 20-dollar bills, $50,000 in 10- dollar bills, $50,000 in five-dollar bills, all of it in Federal Reserve notes and unmarked.

Point 12 of the ransom note instructed the Weyerhaeusers, "In five days or as soon as you have the money; advertise in the *Seattle P-I* personal column. Say 'we are ready.' And sign it, 'Percy Minnie.' "

"You will be notified where to go when the time comes," said point 17. Point 19 was chilling and explicit: "Just follow the rules and you will get along fine. Don't follow them and it will be sorrowful. FOR YOU NOT FOR US."

The ransom note was signed "Egoist."

This brought on the psychiatrists. Dr. Harry R. Hoffman of Chicago studied the ransom note and said Egoist was, "a man unusually well-educated, probably with college training; medically and legally sane; definitely homicidal, if trapped; careful and methodical; with a surprisingly high order of intelligence."

Another psychiatrist, Dr. A. C. Stewart of Tacoma, took his cut at the ransom note. He said that whoever wrote it "was an adult of very low mental grade."

But the cops and the press continued to think of Egoist as a cluster of hoods, the kidnapping as mob-inspired. The kidnapping, they insisted, was the work of ruthless, cunning men.

The kidnappers turned out to be not a gang, or a mob, but three impulsive free-lancers, one of them a woman. The most criminally inclined was William Mahan, also known as Swede Davis, and William Dainard, with a rap sheet of five bank robberies, including a $100,000 heist in Idaho. He had just served a term in prison for bank robbery.

The woman was a somewhat pretty and placid 19-year-old blonde named Margaret Thulin, who had met and married a tall, handsome 24-year-old loser named Harmon Waley, a native of Hoquiam and the third kidnapper. Margaret was from Salt Lake City. Waley had been in and out of reformatories and jails since he was 17 years old, mostly for fighting and drunkenness. He was by no means a hardened criminal, not in the same league with Mahan, a committed tough guy. Harmon Waley was dumber than a box of rocks. His bride was similarly endowed.

That first evening in captivity, George was released from his pit and everyone had a picnic dinner of sandwiches, cookies and hard-boiled eggs. Then George was put back in the pit, handcuffed again, with two blankets and a kerosene lantern.

Cops and G-men indicated this was a carefully researched snatch, as much as three years in the planning by resourceful and experienced criminal minds. Actually, the trio plotted the kidnapping rather impulsively. The three of them were living in Spokane when Margaret happened to read the obituary of John Philip Weyerhaeuser Sr., George's grandfather. The obituary dwelt at some length on the family's wealth. Within three days, Mahan and Waley were casing George's movements as he went to and from school. The precise time of his capture was an accident. They were merely checking out his movements when George emerged from the Tennis Club grounds.

"Where is Stadium Way?" one of the men asked.

The little boy moved closer to the men in the car in order to answer.

One of the men grabbed George, shoved him down on the rear floor of the sedan and told him to keep quiet. In a matter of minutes, the kidnappers made their way out of the city.

Insofar as the kidnappers had any, Mahan was the trio's brains. He was the leader, who dominated Waley and his wife; he was the author of the 21-point ransom letter, a lengthy document that would have earned, perhaps, a C-minus as a grammar school essay. By now, of course, the police had been alerted to George's disappearance, so Mahan's instructions not to call in the law was already breached. George's father, Philip Weyerhaeuser, got the money together and placed his ad in the *P-I*.

Then he added another note: "Due to publicity beyond our control please indicate another method of reaching you. Hurry. Percy Minnie."

George was removed from his pit and taken farther into the woods and entombed in another hole the kidnappers had dug for emergencies. He was chained there for a night and a day. Then the boy was taken out and locked in the trunk of Mahan's car. Holes had been punched in the trunk so George wouldn't suffocate, and he was driven that night clear across the state, some 300 miles, to Spokane. In those days, this would have been a hard trip for a child even if he had been riding in a comfortable seat next to the driver.

George did not complain. He was quiet and he didn't cry. Mahan sometimes jerked him about, but Waley would intervene. They handcuffed George to a tree near the Washington-Idaho border; he was left there a full day while the kidnappers went into Spokane. They came back that night with a large Uneeda cracker carton. The kidnappers packed George into the box and took him to a house they had rented in Spokane.

Life became more comfortable for George. He was locked in a closet in the two-bedroom house at 1509 W. 11th Ave. The house was owned by the Rev. Ella A. Evans, 78, an ordained minister of the Congregational Church. George was shackled in the closet for three days and nights, although Harmon Waley, who watched over him, let the boy walk around freely at times and brought him hot dogs and soft drinks. George was given a mattress to sleep on and Waley slept on another mattress outside the closet door.

Mahan and Margaret raced to Seattle and set up residence at the

Fir Apartments. A second ransom note was sent, at which point the scheme took on elements of melodrama. George's father was instructed to go to the Ambassador Hotel, register under the name of James Paul Jones and await a telephone call. It was not long in coming. Philip Weyerhaeuser was told to drive to a point midway between Tacoma and Seattle. As instructed, he found a stake with a cloth tied to it. A can at the base of the stake held a note directing him to another stake on a dirt road off the highway.

Philip Weyerhaeuser could not find the second stake. About dawn he returned to the Ambassador Hotel. Another phone call came. "Go home and send somebody else with the money," he was told. This time George's uncle, F. Rodman Titcomb, was dispatched to the Ambassador, and from there, by phone, he was sent to a place near the Half Way House, a well-known spot where the Seattle-Tacoma Airport now stands. Titcomb found the stake with a note in a can. The message directed him to a road that bypassed nearby Angle Lake. A second stake and a second note were there.

Titcomb was told to turn on the dome light of his car. He was to put the suitcase with $200,000 cash on the front seat. He was to leave the engine running, leave the car and walk down the dark road.

Mahan and Margaret were parked close by. Mahan piled into Titcomb's car, drove to a shack he had rented on the edge of Seattle and hid the $200,000. He left Titcomb's car on a side street. Margaret drove Mahan's car back to the Fir Apartments; Mahan then retrieved his car and was on his way back to Spokane, even as Titcomb still was walking on a dark road back to town.

Days had passed; George and Waley were getting along nicely. Waley, wearing a hood as a disguise, gave George food and treats, let him walk freely in the house and entertained him, presumably, by playing a ukulele. Waley even gave George newspaper accounts to read about his own kidnapping. Harmon may have been big and stupid, but he was not cruel, unless you count the ukelele.

When Mahan arrived, George again was packed into the car's trunk and taken back to Seattle. Now it was night again. Mahan and Harmon picked up Margaret at the Fir Apartments, drove out to the shack, divided the ransom money and put Margaret on a train to Salt Lake City. Then the men left the city, with George still locked in the trunk. By now it was only a few hours before dawn. They stopped the car on a lonely road near Issaquah.

They got George out of the trunk and one of them told him: "Just walk down this road. Pretty soon your father will come along and give you a ride home. You don't have to be afraid of anything, even if it is dark. Just keep walking this way and you'll get home." There was a pause, then: "You've been a very fine boy."

They gave George two blankets and one dollar. The nine-year-old boy was free.

George had been in captivity for eight days. Northwest readers of newspapers were given some lurid headlines to feast upon. "Posses Speed Kidnap Chase!" cried one. "Clues Point to Kidnappers' Olympic Wilds Hideout" was another. The Karpis gang, out of the Midwest, got a persistent press: "Karpis Mobsters Linked to Crime." Pictures of George were frequent, and one story was headed: "Boy's Radiant, Sunny Smile Would Melt 'Heart of Stone.' " "Call Off G-Men Is Gangsters' Demand." The nation's top cop, J. Edgar Hoover, was in good form. "It may be a day. It may be a week. It may be years before we capture the kidnappers. But we are going to capture them. The long grind has begun," he told the wire services.

Elsie Robinson, a writer known for her magazine fiction, came to Tacoma and set up shop, accompanied by her husband and her secretary. Babette Hughes, the wife of Glenn Hughes, who was head of the University of Washington Drama Department, wrote articles speculating on the kidnapping's solution. The *Seattle Times* reported the arrival of two New York journalists, elegantly dressed and wearing spats.

Newsreel crews, syndicate writers, local reporters, photographers, radio people and curious onlookers virtually surrounded the Weyerhaeuser residence. Seattle and Tacoma police were deluged with calls from all over the nation, mostly from people giving advice on how to trap kidnappers.

While all this was going on, a small, quiet man named Johnny Dreher was working at the *Seattle Times*. He was a golf writer.

Among the Fourth Estate's firmament of stars assigned to the Weyerhaeuser boy's disappearance, the name of Johnny Dreher was least known. In addition to covering club golf matches, Johnny also wrote about trapshooting and sailing. He was 59 years old, settling into a groove of near-retirement. Johnny Dreher never was assigned the big team sports, like Washington Husky football or Seattle Indians baseball. Frequently, on his own, he would arrive at the *Times*' sports department as early as 5 a.m. He would handle some early copy, then lean back in his chair, place a newspaper over his face, and await the regulars, who came in at 7.

The sports editor was George M. Varnell, a towering figure at the *Times*. The paper's city editor was a tough martinet named Ray Felton. The Times' star reporter was Douglass Welch, later of the P-1, who became a nationally syndicated humorist. It was said that Felton fired Welch several times a month, but each morning after being fired, Welch would be back on the job. He never took the firings seriously. Among the *Times*' goodly supply of veteran reporters were a couple of young hands, Henry Macleod, who later would become managing editor, and Vince O'Keefe, a copy boy, who became a top sports reporter and deskman.

Johnny Dreher was a good golf writer, his job was secure, and he enjoyed needling George Varnell. Now and then he would lean back into his chair, a newspaper over his face, and say to Varnell, "I know you're watching me, George. I'm just resting." Or he would counsel young reporters: "You guys are too afraid of Varnell. Don't be afraid of him. He's just a big bag of wind." Everybody liked Johnny Dreher, even Varnell.

During the period of George Weyerhaeuser's disappearance, the byline of Johnny Dreher would appear among the dozens of kidnap stories. This was because Dreher had a private fixation on crime-he liked to read about it in *True Detective* magazine, in *Black Mask*, or in any of a dozen pulp magazines that were popular in those days. In his leisure time he wrote similar stories himself, being an old police reporter. So, *Times* editors let Johnny Dreher out of the office, so he could journey to Tacoma and turn in pieces about the Weyerhaeuser crime.

It was early on Saturday morning, June I, that the kidnappers advised little George Weyerhaeuser that he had been a fine boy, turned him loose and told him to begin walking down the dark road.

Saturday was a big day at the *Times* because that was when

everybody put together the Sunday paper. Johnny Dreher was confined to office work that day because there were no golf matches worth covering, except by telephone.

Dreher was alone in the office when the telephone rang. The caller said he'd received a tip that the Weyerhaeuser boy had been turned loose somewhere near Issaquah. Dreher received another call from the Associated Press saying the same thing. Dreher had a hunch. "It was one of those hunches that come like a royal flush," he said later. Johnny called a taxicab, which happened to be driven by a man named Earl Robinson.

George Weyerhaeuser was still walking down the road when it began to rain. He was not frightened in the darkness, but his blanket was damp, and his feet were wet. About daylight he came upon a shingled house, back from the road a bit and on a grassy knoll. It was the house of John Bonifas, a stump farmer. Mrs. Bonifas was preparing breakfast for her husband and four children. George went around in back and knocked on the kitchen door.

When Mrs. Bonifas opened the door, she saw this bedraggled kid standing there.

"I'm the little boy who was kidnapped," George said.

Mrs. Bonifas hurried George inside. She took off his wet shoes and hung his socks by the stove to dry. She fitted him with a pair of dry shoes that belonged to her daughter. George sat at the table and had his breakfast with the Bonifas family. Afterward, John Bonifas put George in the front seat of his old Model T Ford and began driving along the road that led to Tacoma.

Dreher's taxicab passed them going the other way. "That's the boy, that's the boy," Johnny said. "Turn around and catch them." In a few minutes, Earl Robinson pulled his cab alongside Bonifas and signaled him to stop. George was transferred from the car to Dreher's taxicab, much to the relief, it seemed, of John Bonifas. All John Bonifas said was, "I'll take my little girl's shoes back now."

"Stay away from cars and stay away from people," Dreher told Robinson. He placed George on the back seat, told him to keep down, then covered him with his blanket. Johnny Dreher then settled on the rear floor of the taxicab, pencil and notebook on his lap. He was now developing the biggest newspaper scoop in America.

George told it all. He talked about Waley and Mahan, who wore masks during most of his captivity. He talked about the pits and the shackles and about the long rides in the trunk of the tan Buick. He was never really afraid, George said, except for that time when they passed a river in the woods. "You aren't going to throw me in and drown me, are you?" George asked them. They hurt him only once, he said, and that was by accident, when they pulled him out of the car's trunk.

Much of the time, George said, he was blindfolded. He never knew where he was. Once they told him he was near Aberdeen. On another occasion, they told him he was in Oregon. He never knew that he had been in Spokane. Dreher took copious notes as George talked on.

Once George paused and said, "Mister …? Mister …?"

"It's Dreher," Johnny said, "pronounced like 'prayer.' "

The cab finally reached the Weyerhaeuser mansion overlooking Commencement Bay. Earl Robinson drove his taxicab past the onlookers, the press watchdogs and the photographers. Johnny Dreher took George out of the taxicab and led him up the stairs to the mansion's front door.

The door was opened by a family friend, Marfield Bascom, and Dreher brightened. Bascom, it happened, was a golfing pal and surely, Dreher thought, he would be asked inside and thanked profusely for bringing the boy home. Instead, Bascom pushed Dreher in the face, pulled George inside and slammed the door. Johnny Dreher never saw little George Weyerhaeuser again.

His feelings somewhat bruised, Dreher got back in his taxicab and headed for Seattle. On the way, he stopped to telephone the *Times* that he had picked up the Weyerhaeuser boy and would be in to write his story. When the *Times*' golf writer finally arrived in the newsroom, Col. Clarence B. Blethen, the paper's boisterous, colorful, sometimes obstreperous publisher, was beside himself with joy. His paper, to be sure, had scored an exclusive that dwarfed anything done by the Eastern press and, on this Sunday, it would smother the rival morning *P-I*, owned by the hated William Randolph Hearst, with an exclusive, firsthand account of the kidnapped boy's safe return to his family. Ray Felton, the gifted terrorist of the newsroom, hovered over Johnny Dreher and his typewriter, not as a martinet but as a kindly cohort.

By now the presses were rolling. Dreher's dramatic account was sent in short takes, sometimes only a paragraph in length, sometimes just a sentence, and it would go out to the composing room slugged "18th add Dreher," and "28th and Dreher, more to cum" and finally on up to "40th add Dreher." It was a story full of juice and drama; there was sentiment in it, too, as Johnny Dreher wrote about how he had hugged the Weyerhaeuser boy and kissed him on the cheek. The *Times* even featured a story on Earl Robinson, the cab driver. It carried a deep, two-column picture of balding Johnny Dreher.

By midafternoon the word was out that Johnny Dreher, the little golf writer, was journalism's national hero. Congratulatory calls came from all over America, some from well-known newspaper editors, and the telegrams added up to hundreds. Finally, the *Times*' switchboard operator had to take a break; she burst into the sports department and commandeered Johnny Dreher's chair, and said, "I'll bet he hugged and kissed George, too—the old sentimentalist!" She was Mary Louise Dreher, Johnny's daughter.

It is said that Col. Clarence B. Blethen gave Dreher a bonus on the spot, but nobody remembers that. What they do remember is that the colonel made Dreher the gift of a trip, an all-expenses journey back east to cover the U.S. Open Golf Tournament that summer. This was in itself fairly big news, at least in Seattle. In those Depression days, no editor or publisher in his right mind would finance a golf trip as far away as Everett.

It seems so long ago now, when Tubby Graves waved his bat in front of us kids and said, "If you want to hit the Weyerhaeuser kidnapper in the belly, you do it like this …." I did not know Johnny Dreher, being too young at the time, although I did once work for Henry Macleod and became a good friend and colleague of Vince O'Keefe. About a year after his brief, shining moment in journalism, Johnny Dreher died. It is safe to say that few who work at the *Times* today ever heard of him.

5

The Legend

W ell, one day in August 1991, Harry Givan played 18 holes of golf
with a couple of friends at Seattle Golf and Country Club, which
isn't so unusual by itself. Harry is a member there, having paid his
initiation fee of $900 many years ago, and he often plays with members
who have paid $60,000 to get themselves anointed by the club's board
of admissions, since Seattle G & CC is easily the most exclusive (and
most beautiful) of all Northwest golf courses. Even at $60,000 up front,
the waiting list is longer than the chow line on the USS *Lexington*.

Anyway, Harry shot these 18 holes, keeping everybody's scores
in his head, the way he always does, and when the friendly foursome
ended they went into the bar and knocked back a few. Harry had shot
a 71, a nice enough score but nothing to call the wire services about.

Harry has shot a lot of 71s. He has shot a lot of 68s, some 65s, and
even, on one memorable occasion in 1944, a 61 to set a course record at
Broadmoor. It still remains a record, because they changed the course
right after that by reworking some holes on the back nine.

What made that 71 Harry shot at Seattle in 1991 somewhat special
is that in a few days Harry Givan would celebrate his 80th birthday. He
had finished nine strokes below his age! And he had probably had a
few Scotches before they teed off. He usually does.

To launch from this into an argument that Harry Givan is flat-out
the best athlete the Northwest has ever produced …. Hell, that's about
the size of it.

No other compares. Not Fred Hutchinson, the great baseball
kid, who came out of Franklin High School and later managed St.
Louis and Cincinnati. Not George Wilson, the first authentic Husky

All-American running back of story and legend. We have had basketball stars, baseball greats and near-greats, a few more football All-Americans, Helene Madison, who practically owned the Olympic Games in swimming, a couple of world boxing champions in Al Hostak and Freddie Steele ... but none of them, not one, compares to this golfer we are talking about.

The best athlete ever? A golfer? You know what they say about golfers: "A mailman walks more miles and he carries his own bag."

But let's take a look at this kid before he entered Roosevelt High or the UW. He was a caddy then at Seattle Golf and Country Club. He was part of a kind of "shape up" for caddying jobs, hidden away in the back of the clubhouse. Because he liked golf, he entered a caddies' tournament at Inglewood, out by Kirkland, riding the bus and clutching his bag with a few hickory-handled clubs in it.

He was 11years old. On that day, in 1923, he played in his first tournament. Coming up to the 12th hole at Inglewood, Harry took a deep breath, the way you do before a backswing—and shot a hole in one!

Two years later he beat all the caddies in the city for his first tournament victory. That night he rode back on the streetcars, clutching his little trophy to his chest with both hands, fearful that somebody would steal it from him.

He lived in the north end of town, and downtown Seattle seemed far away. He would catch the interurban train as it came down from Everett and ride to 85th and Greenwood. There he would get off and catch a street car to Pike Street, downtown, then board another streetcar out to Jefferson, the oldest public golf course in Seattle.

But golf wasn't something Harry took very seriously then, except for the 15 cents a round that he earned carrying a member's bag for 18 holes. At Lincoln High he turned out for basketball, baseball and golf. Twice he made all-city in basketball. He made all-city three times in baseball. He also got a minor letter, playing four years on the golf team. He was the first high school player ever to shoot 70 at Jefferson.

In baseball, he was named to the all-city team, first as a shortstop, then as a catcher and finally as a pitcher. In his senior year, Harry Givan went to the Lincoln football coach, Bud Greathouse, and told him he had a problem. Greathouse was once a star football player in his own right—and a mountain climber, who would later lose his life in an avalanche on Mt. Rainier.

Harry said, "I've been getting a little razzing around school. They say that I have no guts, that I play no-contact sports like baseball and basketball and golf, that I don't like to get hit. I want to turn out for football in my last year."

Greathouse nodded, scarcely able to conceal his joy. Never having played football before, Harry became the starting quarterback for Lincoln and played in the first high school game at Civic Field, where the High School Memorial Stadium now stands. He didn't make all-city, but he had made his point.

What his schoolmates didn't know is that Harry took up boxing, quietly, because he didn't want to make noise about it. He did his boxing under an assumed name. He would go down to the old Austin & Salt abattoir at 9th and Olive, where Lonnie Austin and Dan Salt, the two boxing impresarios, had a good thing going. They would sell tickets by having young guys come down and appear on their amateur cards. They would pay a kid $3 if he went the distance, $5 if he scored a knockout and $1 just for showing up. Harry scored 22 knockouts.

These boxing purses kept Harry Givan in spending money and paid for his golf clubs. He would buy his clubs at Spelgier & Herbert, a hardware store on Pike Street. A Hoylake iron, with a hickory shaft, cost $1.49. He paid about the same for a Columbia Special wood. He did not figure he could afford to buy the better clubs at Frederick & Nelson.

There is a creature called a "bird dog" in baseball. A bird dog is a scout who tips off professional baseball men when a kid in some remote area shows promise. One of them watched Harry make all-city those three years at Lincoln High.

The bird dog made a collect call and spoke to Jimmy Caveny, the famous manager of the San Francisco Seals. The Seals, a great institution in their own right, were also a conduit for selling players to the major leagues.

The bird dog said on the phone, "You better get up here, Jimmy. This kid I'm talkin' about is a friggin' pheenom, is what he is."

So Jimmy Caveny got on a train and spent two days getting to Seattle. He offered Harry $250 a month, which in those days, 1929, was a considerable shower of money.

The kid had a nice conversation with the veteran baseball manager. Then Caveny almost fell over when Harry said, in effect, "No, thanks, I think I'll go to school."

In all, Harry Givan counted up 19 scholarship offers he got from colleges and universities. He decided to enter the University of Washington and study business administration. He gave up football, baseball and basketball, which some coaches thought was almost a criminal act against nature because Harry, in addition to his other athletic skills, could run 100 yards in about 10 seconds. Not many humans in the world could do that.

What you had here were the classic ingredients that went into manufacturing a confirmed athlete bum of the 1920s and 1930s. There wasn't much money in being a pro, not in those days, but a kid with an aversion to work could easily sponge around on the semi-pro fringes and maybe set up a pseudo-rich life among the wealthy members of a golf club. But Harry Givan did not want to be a golf bum.

He played some golf, of course. He began shooting some startling scores in and around Seattle—at the privates, like Rainier, Inglewood, Broadmoor, Glendale, and at Tacoma Golf & Country, a historic layout, the first course ever built in the Northwest. He also played on the public courses, like Jefferson, Seattle's first, and Jackson, which came along in the early '30s. At the UW he became captain of the Husky golf team, playing some collegiate matches and a few tournaments. He ran his life on his own terms, and he would say, "I want to be no man's man."

He took an engineering test at Puget Sound Power and Light, passed it, quit the university, then worked three years for the power company. He won the State Amateur in 1933, and again in 1936, but having quit the power company to get into the insurance business, Harry had to live in New York. He would come home to visit his family and, on occasion, to defend his State Amateur title. He'd win the tournament, then fly back to New York on those howling old piston planes, in order to be at work on Monday morning.

While in New York, Harry played the notorious Pine Valley in New Jersey, a spectacular course and a beast to play. He never shot over 72 at Pine Valley. Once he teamed up there with Scotty Campbell, another Northwest golfer, against Johnny Shields and Bobby Jones. Shields was a top pro and Jones, of course, was golf's greatest international figure. The man who founded the Master's Tournament at Augusta was the only golfer ever to win what they called the Grand Slam—the U.S. Open, the British Open, the PGA and the British Amateur. Givan and Campbell beat Jones and Shields, 3 and 2. Harry also took the measure of Sam Snead when Snead was a marquee player and an icon on the professional tour. This was at the Spokane Open in 1942. He won an exhibition match with Byron Nelson. He lost to Jack Nicklaus by one stroke in Ithaca, N.Y., when Nicklaus was a young super player; Nicklaus made a birdie on the 18th hole to win.

In golf the quality of players, as in perhaps no other sport, can be quite accurately compared from one generation to another because they overlap. The old players, the ones who came along in Harry's boyhood, who played with hickory clubs, who shot from high roughs onto tiny greens, developed a shrewd knowledge of the game, with its infinite variety and its infinite pitfalls.

Givan played in the first of six consecutive national amateur championships in Brookline, Massachusetts, in 1934. He was a big man, a solid 215-pounder, six feet tall, and when they got a look at him in Brookline, a Boston paper called him "the Babe Ruth of golfers." This was after he hit one drive that measured 327 yards off the tee.

It was a funny career, really, because for the most part Harry played only when and where he could, in tournaments that he could fit into his business schedule. "Golf," he would tell people, "has never been the alpha and omega of my life," and he has played only what he called "catch-as-catch-can" golf since 1930.

He won the Seattle City Amateur four times and the Northwest and Washington State Amateurs five times each. He won numerous opens. He won the Seattle Golf Club Championship 10 times. On the day Givan destroyed Broadmoor with a record-setting 61, the noted crooner and golf buff Bing Crosby was in the audience.

"What a golfer!" exclaimed Crosby. "I could take him through Texas with a bag of clubs, a chuck-a-luck game, and a balloon dancer, and we'd have all the money in the state."

Golf was always Harry's fun game. "Don't take it too seriously," was his credo. "Play it squarely and fairly with good manners, and everything will be all right."

Now, at 80, he plays only when the weather is right and with people he likes. To this day, he will have maybe three Scotches at lunch, then hit his first drive, and every drive thereafter, straight and true down the middle of the fairway. Then perhaps a golf cart will pass him on the way and somebody will yell, "Nice going, Legend." The ultimate tribute.

6

The Man Who Left the Door Open

There was kind of a haphazard nobility about him, although he would never aspire to that, even if he was of English stock, even if his forebears did come over long before a Revolutionary War occurred to anybody. In his own favorite phrase, he became a "typical punkerino." He was born at 28th and Yesler, one mile from the hospital in which he died. He was a true Seattle native, even a semi-pioneer.

Being a punkerino, he worked at almost everything and in 1917, when the United States entered what his generation called the Great War, he "couldn't wait to get over to France and save the world for democracy." He enlisted in the Army Engineers in the basement of the Pioneer Building at James and Occidental because the Engineers promised him immediate combat.

He finished only his second year at Broadway High. He never learned the multiplication tables, but he had the savvy to help run the City of Seattle as a dynamic councilman and frequent acting mayor.

If you have nothing more uplifting to do, go down to the Municipal Building on Fourth Avenue and there you will see his name inscribed along with those of other councilmen of the early 1950s: Alfred Rochester. They didn't have room for his middle initial.

He spent 12 years on the City Council, and to his dying breath Al Rochester did not like the Municipal Building. He raised a sizeable fuss about it, saying that it should be bigger and of better quality, that proper bids were not let on it and that the architects, one of whom was the celebrated B. Marcus Priteca, were only one rung more exalted than hod carriers. Al always spoke his mind.

I remember a picture of Al, run in some magazine, in which he looked like one of the landed English gentry. He was wearing a tweed jacket, a woven cloth cap with a hard bill, horn-rimmed glasses, a rough outdoors shirt, and a splendid, neatly trimmed white mustache. He also wore a stem expression, mouth pulled down, face looking truculent.

The stern expression was not part of Rochester's usual demeanor. He was, to the contrary, open, friendly, democratic and funny. He seemed to know everybody in Seattle, from working stiffs to Rainier Clubbers. And he was the man who opened the door to the Seattle World's Fair of 1962.

To understand Al Rochester, you have to know how the city was run in those days. Back in the 1940s and '50s and even into the '70s, Seattle had a weak-mayor system. The City Council packed most of the clout.

There was much less public input than we are used to now; meetings often were held behind closed doors, and big decisions could be made privately over drinks.

This was not always bad. When Al was head of the Streets and Sewers Committee, the city got up $370,000 to install mercury vapor street lights. They put some in the high-crime areas and took care of the more affluent neighborhoods, and everything was fine.

Then one day a woman came into Al's office and told him that Chinatown—that's what we called it then—had been slighted.

"The Chinese are very upset," she said. "They live on King Street and the city put lights in other areas, but not theirs. They are hurt."

So, Al saw the woman politely to the door, then called the city engineer. "How's our money on vapor lights?" he asked. The engineer said, "Well, there's a street out on Nineteenth Avenue by the Isaac I. Stevens School and the people out there don't want lights. So, we've got about sixteen thousand dollars left."

"All right," said the majestic chairman of Streets and Sewers, "don't tell anybody and don't try any special legislation. Just stick it in the next bill that comes through my committee, but for Chrissakes put lights up on King Street!"

Al Rochester was a charter member of the Pittypat Club, which met once a week, usually, at one of those big round tables always found in Chinese restaurants. Present would be three or four councilmen—

maybe Dave Levine, Bob Jones, Mike Mitchell, Bob Harlan and Al Rochester. Mrs. F. F. Powell was the only woman on the council; she was not invited to the Pittypat Club.

The Pittypatters also would include a department head or two, and often the chief of police: Jimmy Lawrence, or Frank Ramon or George Eastman.

These luncheons were good fellowship events where policies were agreed upon in a convivial way without the bother of asking citizens what they wanted.

Well, on the council in those days was a pleasant, round little fellow called "Streetcar" Charlie Carroll. His nickname came from his professional past as a Seattle streetcar motorman. Carroll was a warm, affable and honest politician of the old school. It was said that he got campaign funds from the dubious pinball interests, but then who didn't? So, one day Al Rochester was confronted by Streetcar Charlie in the hallway.

"Why don't you invite me to some of these lunches?" Carroll demanded, and there was hurt in his voice. "I don't know what is going on around here. You pittypat into Levine's office, you pittypat into Mitchell's office, you pittypat into Harlan's office. But you never come around to tell me things. I am not invited to those lunches."

Forever after, the lunchtime get-togethers were known as the Pittypat Club. In later years the locale was moved to Vito's, a marvelous hangout at Ninth and Madison where the bar was three-deep in lawyers, deputy sheriffs, city bureaucrats, politicos and sports fans. If you wanted to sue somebody, have your appendix out or get advice about race horses, that was the place to find specialty help.

The Pittypat Club exists to this day. It meets every Wednesday at Vito's, although the only decisions made now are about how to split the check.

Al Rochester served on the Council from 1948 to 1956. There was a rough-edged sort of get-along-go-along atmosphere around City Hall in those days and, as Al was fond of saying, "You don't have to be crooked to help a guy get a job." On occasion intra-Council beefs went public, as when Rochester called in the press and denounced Mike Mitchell, who owned the *Ballard News-Tribune*, for leaving early to get out the next issue of his weekly paper just as an important measure came to a vote.

But most of the arguments were private. There was the occasion when Council President Levine failed to recognize Rochester during a meeting and then called him out of order. Later, Al stormed into Levine's office.

"Dave, you dirty Lithuanian sonofabitch," Al roared. "If you ever do that to me again, I'm going to walk up on the platform and punch you in the nose."

A broad smile brightened Levine's moody countenance. "Aw, what the hell, Al," he said, "go get us some ice and we'll have a drink."

When Rochester returned with the ice, Levine pulled out the office bottle and things became all right again. As acting mayor, Al took his duties seriously. When he got a harried call one Sunday morning and was told, "The mayor of Minneapolis is arriving down at the Great Northern Depot at 8 o'clock," Al hurried down to greet him.

He didn't know the mayor on sight, so he went to two or three porters and asked the same question: "Anybody get off this train that looks like he might be the mayor of Minneapolis?"

Finally, one porter pointed to a man and woman standing alone, looking puzzled, and that was the beginning of Al's friendship with Hubert Humphrey and his wife, Muriel.

Seattle and Al Rochester knew one another for nearly 100 years. Al was born on a rainy Thursday in March 1895, just six years after Washington achieved statehood. He died in February 1989, the year of Washington's centennial. When he said, "I guess just about everything that happened here happened in my lifetime," it was no idle boast.

When Rochester was born, Seattle had 60,000 people and, as he once said, "You could come out of the Hoge Building and walk for fifteen minutes in any direction and be out of town."

Deer often were seen in backyards; it was common to have a family cow.

Al's childhood home still stands at 28th and Yesler, but in those days 28th was called Rochester Avenue after Al's father, Judge G. A. C. Rochester, a civic power and a strong Baptist of the Southern persuasion.

As a small boy, Al would meet his father in front of the Merchants Cafe in Pioneer Square and ride home with him on the Yesler cable car.

He remembered one trip when his father, the judge, sat next to Hiram Gill, the mayor, who lived in the Rochester neighborhood. Mayor Gill ran a wide-open seaport town, complete with saloons, brothels and gambling. Al remembered his Baptist father shaking his finger under Gill's nose and proclaiming, "Hiram, what you are doing is not right, you know it's not right!"

Al learned to cuss and, later, to drink. But he always kept that bone-in Baptist ethic that firmly located the dividing line between what was right and what was wrong. They called Seattle's Skid Road the Tenderloin then.

They called it a lot of things: Maynardtown, Lava Beds, Wappyville (after a police chief), but the name that stuck was Skid Road. Later this was bowdlerized into Skid Row and came to mean any city's poor, tough district. The Merchants Cafe, where young Al met his father to catch the cable car, was right in the middle of it.

In that raffish neighborhood the kid delivered the weekly *Argus*, the *Saturday Evening Post* and the local papers. He picked up his magazines and papers in the lobby of the Central Building. "The gambling joints and the whorehouses were all running full blast then," he would recall, "and I would go down to the lower end there and, hell, I would clean up, and then I'd have to walk home at night because the streetcars weren't running that late."

Al was long-legged but supple. He became adept at slipping under swinging saloon doors to peddle papers. When the kid would go into one of his favorite saloons, the bartender would rap the passed-out drunks on the soles of their boots and growl, "Wake up and buy a paper from the kid."

Al Rochester was 14 years old in 1909 when the Alaska-Yukon-Pacific Exposition opened where the University of Washington is today. Al shilled for the exhibits. He sold fresh water. He ran a bread-cutting machine. He was half-blinded by the excitement and glitter of it all, and this thing—this Alaska-Yukon-Pacific Exposition—took hold of him and he could talk for hours about it. His fixation would one day change his whole city, the growing, struggling, brawling, cheap, corrupt, provincial, isolated, waterfront town—a last frontier, for heaven's sake! It would change all of that, for better or worse.

When Al Rochester finished digging trenches and burying bodies in the Argonne and the Marne, those slaughter-house battlefields of World War I, he came back and threw himself on the job market.

He did everything. He shipped out on the American Mail Line to the Orient. He worked on New York's Wall Street, selling bonds, and he would look up at the tall buildings of the city, a place of wealth and power, and he would say to himself, "How can I get a piece of this?"

He came back home, sold more bonds out of an office in the Hoge Building and took up a lively life in the Seattle of the 1920s, where almost everything went. He ushered at the Moore Theater, starred in Junior League shows, went to dances at Faurot Hall on Pine and Broadway. Hey, dancing, that was it!—and the nights slipped past at the Butler Hotel, to the music of Vic Meyers' orchestra.

He made a Seattleite's usual pilgrimage to Manca's, looked for friends at Rippe's, which later became Von's. He gambled and drank at Doc Hamilton's up on 12th.

At the bottom of the 1930s Depression, Al went back to New York City. One day, on 42nd Street on his way down to Times Square, he had this hunch. He went into the New York Times Building and wrote out an ad that said something like this:

"Young man well acquainted and available on the Pacific Coast, specifically Pacific Northwest. Public relations, good connections."

Unbelievable! Some people from New Jersey called him (they never had been west of the Potomac) and paid his expenses to their Virginia headquarters. There he found out that his job was hustling restaurant concessions. Without even signing a contract, Al went calling in California, then up in Washington where he cracked a big one! Boeing. He got the restaurant concession at Boeing's Plant One out on the Duwamish.

All of this time, Al Rochester was getting closer to politics. He became what he called "a top-of-the-hill Democrat." This was not a flip phrase, because in the Seattle of those times, it would have taken a highly competent golden retriever to sniff out any Democrat living on Capitol Hill.

Al had been a precinct committeeman in the '20s. When the New Deal arrived in the '30s and the Democrats came in to power, he was in line for patronage jobs. He was named to head several government agencies and operated out of the U.S. District Courthouse. Every week he would go down to the Northern Life Tower and broadcast on radio about government programs. He answered only to the White House.

One particular evening, at a Democratic precinct meeting of the 37th District, there was a knock on the door and Harry Martin, a committeeman, went to answer it. There was a little conversation and Al called out, "Who is it, Harry?"

Martin closed the door and returned to the meeting. "It's a young guy out there and he wants to be a Democrat. He thought this was a meeting he could join."

"Well, he can't get in this meeting," Al said. "Tell him to go and get himself elected a precinct committeeman and then he can come." So, Martin carried the message back. When he returned, Al asked, "What was the guy's name?"

"He said his name was Magnuson, Warren Magnuson," Martin said. Al would become a good friend of young Magnuson and, a few elections later, became one of Senator Magnuson's confidants and political aides.

The career of Al Rochester, to state it baldly, could scarcely be imagined in today's tidily organized society. His curriculum vitae would drain blood from the cheeks of any proper personnel manager, and yet it was Al's proud boast that he never really asked for a job or ever got fired from one. He got dis-elected once, in 1956, when some dimwit Democrats wouldn't give him campaign money. "Aw, hell, Al, everybody knows you, you don't need to campaign," they said.

In his 12 years on the Seattle City Council, Al, as chairman of Streets and Sewers, had a lot to do with building the Alaskan Way Viaduct; he was instrumental in establishing daylight saving time here; he proposed and effected one-way streets and special street parking for the physically handicapped.

Al Rochester was an idea man and, heaven knows, Seattle needed ideas in the 1950s. Seattle had a quaint but crumbling Pike Place Market, a ratty-looking Civic Auditorium, a Civic Ice Arena with all the ambience of a dungeon, along with a bunch of happy hooligans running around in pirate costumes during the August Seafair.

Seattle was nobody's most livable city. The symphony conductor, Milton Katims, had to present his orchestra in the Orpheum Theatre, an old movie house. The University of Washington football team was a doormat trying to recover from a recruiting and payoff scandal. Excitement, what there was of it, centered on some hydroplane races on Lake Washington. Sometimes the minor-league baseball Rainiers would absent-mindedly go on a winning streak. But for real action, as someone suggested, "you had to go out and do a little illegal fishing."

City concerns fixed on Children's Orthopedic Hospital fund-raising drives, the Ryther Child Center, the debutantes' Christmas Ball and unneutered pets. After the wide-open, sinfully interesting 1920s and 1930s, the Seattle of the '50s settled down to being a city of Babbitry and half-hearted boosterism, eye-smarting charcoal smoke rising from back-yard barbecues, and citizens who meekly watched as highball glasses were snatched off their tables at midnight on Saturdays.

Dr. Mamie Mclafferty did a brisk business in abortions in a building on Pine Street, across from Frederick &. Nelson, but well-off women who got careless could fly to Japan because Japan Airlines was offering a package travel deal: airline fare, room, board and abortion.

"The scenery is great, but the cast is lousy," comedian Joe Frisco said of Seattle then. And it was true. The city didn't rank itself high on its own scale of self-esteem, always comparing itself unfavorably with San Francisco.

Al Rochester still got around a lot, from City Hall to the Washington Athletic Club, even to the Rainier Club when his old friend Henry Broderick took him there. He would make an occasional foray into the Italian Club on Union. In 1932 Al had married a local beauty named Marguerite. She had a job selling real estate for West & Wheeler. They had a son, Junius, and a daughter, Mary Ellen.

One day, Al heard himself saying, "Why don't we have a world's fair?" The former kid shill at the Alaska-Yukon-Pacific Exposition had never got over the enchantment a 14-year-old could experience around exhibits, famous people, dancers, bands, good food and well ... excitement. He had never shaken the energy and joy of those A-Y-P days.

So out loud at lunch one day at the Washington Athletic Club he said, "Why don't we have a world's fair? Let's shoot for 1959, then it'll be a 50th anniversary thing for the Alaska-Yukon-Pacific Exposition."

There were four of them there, and it needs to be noted that at this time the three-martini lunch was popular. Which may explain why none of the other three, Ross Cunningham of the *Seattle Times*, Don Follett of the Chamber of Commerce and a businessman named Denny Givens, suggested that they throw a net over their companion. Instead, Cunningham said that if the idea got airborne, the *Times* would support it editorially, but Follett said the Chamber should not get out too far in front. He said the labor unions would stiff-arm the idea because they'd figure somebody was trying to get rich. And Cunningham said, "It has to be done 'officially' in a way that makes it sound all right." Then Al said, "I'm an official. Just a lousy council man, but still official." That afternoon Rochester went down to the courthouse and got A. C. Van Solen, the city's corporation counsel, to figure out how to write an Alaska-Yukon-Pacific Exposition "memorial" resolution calling for a Seattle world's fair in 1959. The next thing anybody knew, Al got his resolution through the City Council, which was only too happy to accommodate something that wasn't going to cost anything. Well, the idea then went public and in record-breaking time it became a runaway joke.

Especially down at Victor Rosellini's 610 Restaurant, a favored watering place for press agents, newspaper people, artists, creative advertising types and other assorted non-Establishment cynics. A world's fair-in Seattle? The boys put the laugh track up loud and on fast forward. At Victor's lunch rituals, they cut some beautiful wisecracks about the knee-pants notion that a Seafair -prone former fishing village, stuck out here in the rain latitudes, could actually pull off a world's fair. There were some big grins, all right.

None of this fazed Rochester. Al was a booster at heart and he went to work lobbying the State Legislature and, of course, there were his friends, among them Sen. Warren Grant Magnuson, back in D.C. Seattle didn't know much about Eddie Carlson then, but Eddie was an up-from-the-ranks executive in what was then known as Western Hotels, with a streak of gambler in him. Eddie was only a few years removed from testing doorknobs and counting lost hotel keys, but he got caught up in the idea of a world's fair in Seattle.

Eddie was persuasive. Pretty soon they had a World's Fair Commission, and Alfred Ruffner Rochester became its executive director. In remarkably short time some money began to come in-the state put up $7.5 million. Meanwhile, Bob Block, a city activist, had fronted for a$ 7.5 million bond issue to create a Seattle Center out by the Ice Arena.

As it turned out, Carlson became chairman of the Fair Commission, and along came Harold Shefelman, an unctuous bond attorney, to be chairman of the Civic Center Advisory Committee. Later, Carlson would become president of the Century 21 Exposition, the eventual and official name of what drew so much derision around town. But the grandiose title "World's Fair" hung on because Rochester and his fellow instigators wanted to make it sound big when they went after appropriations, exhibits and status.

The laugh track got turned up even louder when somebody got the bright idea to hire Tex McCrary. If anybody could get Seattle's fair some global attention, it would be Tex, who had multimillion-dollar accounts and a spectacular track record as a publicist. McCrary was surprised, but not speechless, when they called him.

"A world's fair? In Seattle?" he said. "Frankly, I've always thought of Seattle as a place where the town prostitute has a pull-down bed."

That was a thigh-slapper, all right. So, when the boys called for their Beefeaters down at the 610 bar, and when Al dropped by on occasion, he got the old razzeroo. He didn't mind particularly, because Al, who had worked on newspapers and once had published his own magazine, *Seattleite*, was almost one of them.

The Seattle World's Fair did come off, just as Al thought it would. Fifty-nine nations were represented. Seattle got introduced to Belgian waffles and Mongolian steaks, press credentials were given to 1,163 reporters from 12 countries, and by the time Century 21 opened on April 21, 1962, Anne Swensen, a press coordinator, had logged 876 stories in magazines with a combined circulation of 200 million.

Century 21 went on full blast for 184 days. Big-name entertainers arrived, along with Prince Philip and even John Wayne, and everybody just had to go up the Space Needle. When they counted it all up, 10 million people had paid to see Seattle's World's Fair and, "second category" or not, the loans got paid off, the fair made money and Seattle Center was bulging with improvements, including a new Coliseum and an Opera House recycled out of the drab old Civic Auditorium, a splendid place, just as Minoru Yamasaki had said it would be.

It came to an end on a cool October night when 20,000 people assembled in Memorial Stadium to witness the closing ceremonies. No fewer than 1,600 bandsmen gathered on the stadium floor while Patrice Munsel, the opera star, sang "Auld Lang Syne," accompanied by Jackie Souders' orchestra, and big Joe Gandy banged down his gavel to bring Century 21 to its official conclusion. "And then," as Dave Hughbanks, the young coordinator of special events, would say, "we went back to being a small town again."

Well, maybe. Al Rochester was always a booster, always a joiner, always upbeat. Civic do-goodism had always been, and continued to be, part of his life.

Then, into the 1970s and through most of the 1980s, Al Rochester settled down to the serious business of growing old. He and Marguerite spent more and more time in a modest vacation home they owned on Whidbey Island. Al would come into town, mostly to socialize, and he would pay a visit now and then to his old Pittypat Club at Vito's.

Al slowed up a bit. In his later years his son, Junius, would drive him around on errands and visits and, of course, Al would meet a lot of people who liked to reminisce about Century 21. Because the fair had been such a resounding success, a milestone in the history of Seattle, there were people whose memories expanded into fantasies about the big event. And some of these people, especially after knocking back a couple, actually believed that they had more or less invented Century 21, that they had had the idea in the first place.

Al didn't care. But once in a while, just for fun, he would tell the story about a man who desperately needed a dime for a pay toilet. Another gent in the men's room gave the man a dime. But, as it happened, the man found a door already open, so he got in free. As Al told it, the man invested his dime wisely and eventually ran it up into a sizeable fortune.

And people would say, "Gee whiz, you certainly are obligated to that guy who gave you the dime." The man would say, "No, I'm obligated to the guy who left the door open."

Al would tell this story when people claimed credit for Century 21, they knew it all along, they were responsible for it, and so forth. Al would listen and then he would say, "Maybe so, but I left the door open for you guys."

7

Yeoman of the Old Guard

O ne lovely spring day in 1949 Charley McIntyre and his brother Joe were single-sculling in the Montlake Cut, the narrow strip of water that joins Lake Washington with Lake Union. No boats had passed through the cut recently, so the water was smooth, and Charley could hear the cars crossing the iron-gridded Montlake Bridge above. It was a perfect day for sculling and Charley was very good at it.

The brothers were from Pennsylvania, where Charley had rowed for the famous Vesper Boat Club. In a way they were anomalies to rowing because their parents did not have much money. Their father worked as a union organizer. Traditionally, rowing is for young men from well-to-do families, but the Vesper Boat Club had accepted Charley because Charley was good—so good, in fact, that he almost had qualified for the U.S. Olympic rowing team in 1948. One of Charley's good friends and a fellow oarsman was Jack Kelly, son of a Philadelphia millionaire and brother of the future Princess Grace of Monaco.

Charley and Joe came to Seattle because their older brother, Dick, played football at the University of Washington. The waters of Seattle-water everywhere-appealed to Charley's love of rowing, and now, at 27, he knew that he never would return to Philadelphia. Charley, being heavy-set and broad-shouldered, was powerful in a single scull. But this was for fun and, because it was spring, and the blood was warm, Charley upped the beat a little, kind of half-racing his brother Joe.

They often did this, Charley and Joe. The brothers had won three U.S. titles rowing as a pair without coxswain.

Abruptly, off to their left, came another single scull. The oarsman was an older man. He appeared to be in his 60s, and as he moved his boat swiftly through the calm waters of the Montlake Cut his gray hair fluttered in the breeze. He pulled even with Joe and Charley, not glancing their way, but to Charley it seemed, in some strange way, that the older man was trying to impart a message to them.

Charley raised his stroke again. The handsome, gray-haired man, sitting erect in his boat, stayed with the other two shells. It got competitive. Charley raised the stroke once more, pulling hard on the oars for 50 meters. The old man was still there. Charley thought, "This old guy has got to cave in pretty soon." Charley raised the stroke once more. Another 50 meters. Now they were out of the Montlake Cut, entering Lake Washington, and Charley thought, "That should do it, that old man doesn't belong with us."

But the gray-haired oarsman stayed even, then pulled ahead of his younger rivals. Charley and Joe were astonished. The old man turned away and went on with his sculling. Years later, Charley would tell this story many times and he would half apologize for being so corny, but he would say, "That was the day I found God in a boat."

The older oarsman, as Charley learned very quickly, was a magnificent man, who had a magnificent middle name. He was George Yeoman Pocock.

In the years to come books would be written about George Yeoman Pocock. He became a legend in the international sport of rowing, and rowing is international—it thrives in England, all of Europe, Russia, much of America and parts of Asia, Australia and South America. In his own time George Pocock made Seattle the spiritual center of rowing. He worked his magic out of an ugly building, scarcely more than a Quonset hut, in a remote corner of the University of Washington campus, at the edge of the Montlake Cut. Because of him, Seattle became a rowing mecca for generations of oarsmen the world over.

Using woods of the Northwest—Alaska spruce and Western red cedar—George Pocock built racing shells of unmatched functional beauty. For many years, Pocock boats dominated crew racing. Many are still in use around the world. A Pocock masterpiece, as carefully crafted as a Stradivarius, is 61 feet long, 23 ¾ inches wide 9 ½ inches deep. Using one of Pocock's shells, University of Washington oarsmen won five straight intercollegiate races in the late 1920s and early 1930s.

"Its beauty defies description," said one rowing expert. "New, it is the color of old ivory. Exposed to light, it deepens into a golden, honeylike hue." Western red cedar, George Pocock said, "is the wood eternal."

Pocock had mastered his art on the Thames River. His father and his father's father were English boat-builders, superb, exacting craftsmen. George was indentured to his father at the age of 14, when English free education stopped. He learned to build boats. And he learned to row by watching the watermen on the Thames-rowing professionals who plied the wherries, "the taxi boats of the Thames," as they ferried passengers up and down and across the river. Since the early 1700s Thames watermen had competed in races, often for big purses. They arranged professional rowing matches the way prize fights were arranged a century later. Bets were posted, and odds quoted among backers of the best oarsmen on earth. This was the environment that produced George Pocock.

He rowed in his first race at the age of 12. He won his first race at the age of 15 and, at the age of 17, he won fifty pounds against some of England's best professional oarsmen.

George needed the fifty pounds. His father had lost his job at Eton College and times were hard. George and his brother Dick could not find work, so they booked steerage to Canada. Eventually, they came to Vancouver, B.C., where they labored in logging camps and then began building boats for the Vancouver Rowing Club. They set up shop in an abandoned shed, one that actually floated and went up and down with the tides in Vancouver's Coal Harbor. They began turning out single and double shells.

Word of their skill spread. Then one day an outlandish visitor arrived.

A half gale was blowing on Coal Harbor and the stranger, laboring hard in a dinghy, rowed his way toward the Pococks' workplace. His coattail flew in the wind, he rocked from side to side, and George remembered, "He was floundering over his oars like a bewildered crab." Dick said, "The fool must be drunk."

They helped the stranger aboard. He had shaggy brows and a wild mop of red hair. "My name is Hiram Conibear," he announced. "I am the rowing coach at the University of Washington in Seattle."

The brothers were incredulous. This apparition, this clumsy

fellow with oars and a dinghy-a crew coach? Only their strict English upbringing kept the Pococks from bursting into laughter.

Conibear brushed them aside and looked around the shop. "Singles and doubles!" he snorted. "Forget them. Come with me to Seattle and you will build eights. Do you hear? Eights! Fifty of them!"

It was the siren call of the true huckster. Conibear was indeed the rowing coach at Washington. He himself did not know how to row, but he was obsessed with establishing rowing as a major sport. So, he conned people. He pleaded with them to be part of his crew program. He had no money for the Pococks to build 50 eight-oared shells; he didn't have the money for even one. But Connie was a con man, adept at raising money and filled with imagination.

He scrounged a human skeleton from a campus laboratory, put it erect on a bench, and tried to figure out the mechanics of rowing from the assembled bones. When his crews practiced on Lake Washington, Connie would run along the shore, yelling instructions through a megaphone; he might climb a tree in order to see better, impatiently swearing at the top of his voice. The neighbors complained to University authorities, who ordered Connie to stop bellowing near the waterfront houses.

This was the improbable pied piper the Pocock brothers followed to Seattle. Conibear, the exuberant salesman, took George out to view the city.

"See these trees," he enthused. "Someday they will all be gone. New and bigger buildings will come. See that water? See that twenty-mile lake? That's Lake Washington. The narrow strip of water is Portage Bay. Over there is Lake Union, three miles long, a mile across, protected from the wind. Someday there will be great tall buildings here. What a city! What a place! You must come here!"

George and his brother Dick succumbed. They built Washington's first eight-oared shell in 1912. Overcoming profound lack of interest in crew racing as a sport, Connie succeeded in getting the University to send his eight-oared shell to the big collegiate regatta at Poughkeepsie. It was a remarkable feat of salesmanship. Even more surprising was the untested Conibear crew's finish, a close third behind Syracuse and Cornell. In Seattle this was big stuff, and civic booster pride opened wider the city's pocketbooks to Conibear and his beloved rowing.

Gently, politely, George Pocock tried to impart his racing knowledge to the boisterous Conibear, the man who could not row himself. He succeeded, in part, and as Washington rowing continued, a strange myth began to arise about a thing called "the Conibear stroke." That's all it was—a myth, a congenial fraud. Asked about it at the time, Rusty Callow, a great Washington oarsman, said, "Well … the Conibear stroke, it seems to change every year." Even Connie didn't understand it. When people asked him to define the Conibear stroke, he would shrug and say, "It's the stroke that gets you there."

A seminal moment in Washington's great rowing tradition came when a remarkable young man named Ed Leader, a No. 2 oar in one of Conibear's boats, came to George Pocock after an especially awkward practice on Lake Washington.

"Mr. Pocock," Ed Leader said, "there's got to be a better way to do this."

George listened to Leader's plea, but he hesitated. He was not a man to push himself forward; he was imbued with British reticence and he was, after all, a builder of shells, not a rowing coach. And he had come to love Hiram Conibear for his almost messianic crusade to establish rowing at Washington. He did not want to hurt Connie.

But finally, after a long pause, George Pocock answered Ed Leader. "There is a better way," he said.

Gradually, with what amounted to a genius for quiet persuasion, Pocock began to implant into Washington's young oarsmen the ancient rowing lore he had learned on the Thames. He passed along the legacy of nearly 200 years of professional British rowing, as practiced by watermen who earned their living with efficient use of oars. He quietly urged his wisdom on Conibear and, through Connie, some of it filtered down to the eights.

In 1916, the beloved Conibear came to a sad end. While pruning a fruit tree in his back yard, Connie fell to his death. The loss hit everyone hard. But it was an ironically propitious moment for Washington crews. The way was now clear for Pocock to coach.

Pocock would coach, yes, but he would do so only through young surrogates. Pocock admired Rusty Callow, a No. 7 oar on a Conibear eight. With the job now vacant, Pocock urged the University to put Callow in charge, and it agreed.

The boats began to go faster with less effort; they developed rhythm and poise, and with refined skills came confidence. A Washington boat became eight oars pulling as one.

George Pocock was showing them a better way.

In 1923 the Washington varsity and freshman crews, under Rusty Callow, journeyed to the Hudson River for another try at the Poughkeepsie Regatta. They never had won there in eight years. Callow insisted on taking Pocock along.

In the elite Eastern rowing establishment of 1923, Washington was not regarded as a threat. Few at the seaboard schools had ever heard of Pocock, much less Rusty Callow.

But suddenly it was different. These were not the bumpkins of early years; they were a smooth, crisp, elegant crew. They had the strength and know-how to make a cedar shell burst with power.

When the race began, Columbia broke in front, followed by Navy, Cornell, Syracuse—then Washington and Wisconsin. With a mile to go, Navy shot ahead. Rowing precisely, confidently, almost effortlessly, Washington moved ahead of Cornell. The Huskies passed Columbia, again without seeming effort; at the finish line, they knifed across in front of Navy. It was an unprecedented upset—who are these guys? Washington. The crew from the Far West had soundly beaten the best in the East.

George remembered the Easterners asking, "Where is Seattle? Tell us, Mister, we never heard of the place." Washington's rowing boys had brought along a few small totem poles to hand out as souvenirs. The Easterners were convinced: "Good God, they're from Indian country!"

George and Rusty came home to a heroes' welcome. Mayor Edwin "Doc" Brown gave a speech and all the City Council bustled about, proud to be near the victorious athletes. Big time! Big stuff! The mouth-breathing downtown boosters couldn't get enough of crew racing now. In later years, when the Huskies rowed at home on Lake Washington, as many as 100,000 people lined the shores.

A tradition was growing down at the shell house where Pocock fashioned those bright, skinny, eight-oared shells, boats so light and water-worthy that their crews were able to clip seconds off previous records. More and more young men came to Washington to try out for crew. Often there were five or six boatloads of them, freshmen and sophomores earnestly trying to earn a place. Many failed and were turned away.

They were tough kids, these early Washington oarsmen. They did not come from privileged families like many you would find at Harvard, Yale, Rutgers and Princeton. The Washington boys were used to hard work; they were kids who had saved their money to get an education. They came out of logging camps, they had pulled nets on purse seiners, they had worked in the wheat fields of eastern Washington, they had labored on construction crews and in apple orchards and on dairy farms. They were so hard and lean that Charley McIntyre would later observe, "You could roller skate on their backs."

When sportswriter Royal Brougham called the crews "the tall firs from the Northwest," people smiled and said, "Oh, that's just Royal waxing poetic." But it was true. These kids were noticeably larger than their Eastern counterparts. Crew was endless hard work? So be it. When you have bucked wheat in 100-degree weather or worked 24-hour days on a salmon trawler, everything after that seems easy.

Washington crews under Rusty Callow began to dominate American rowing. They won again at Poughkeepsie in 1924; they were nipped by Navy in 1925 but swept the Hudson once more in 1926.

Callow himself was a robust product of a logging family from the Olympic Peninsula. When he took his crews to Poughkeepsie, and the Eastern rowing fans and writers gathered to watch him work with his oarsmen, Rusty would have a chaw of tobacco in his cheek. Then he would let one go.

Those who knew Rusty well smiled a bit. Rusty, they thought, was showing off; but this also was his way of telling people what he was and where he came from.

There were little slights at Poughkeepsie. Nothing you could define, really, just a glance, perhaps an inflection of the voice. These Eastern crews were polite enough, but still … they had a way about them, they knew an appleknocker when they saw one. Just little things, like turning away to smile at a Husky's way of using a dinner fork. Sometimes it was blatant, out in the open; one Eastern paper scoffed at Washington's "clumsily built Western shells."

The kids read that, and when it came time to race, they wanted the victory even more—and got it.

Washington's dominance lasted for only a few years. Then the Eastern schools, awakened to the new rowing power from the Northwest, took counter-measures. They began hiring Washington graduates, trained under Pocock and Callow, young men scarcely a year or two out of college.

Ed Leader went to Yale and with him he took George Pocock's brother, Dick. Ky Ebright, a shrewd Washington coxswain, became head coach at California. Tom Bolles was hired to revive the Harvard crews. Stork Sanford went away to Cornell; later on, Norm Sonju became the coach at Wisconsin.

Then Rusty Callow himself. Not Rusty? Yes! Pennsylvania offered Callow an unheard-of salary for a crew coach—$20,000 a year. Unbelievable!

By now Pocock had become the prophet of Washington rowing. School authorities, wealthy alums, former oarsmen came to the shell house where George, always in coveralls, turned out those shells. What do we do now? Rusty's gone! Who can replace him?

"Al Ulbrickson," George said.

Ulbrickson had been a powerful stroke oar on Callow's great crews of 1924, 1925 and 1926. Ulbrickson was a Northwest son of hard-working Danish parents, and, because he disciplined his emotions and gazed at the world with cold gray eyes, Eastern writers dubbed him "the Dour Dane." The cliché "ice water in his veins" was often used. But those who came to know him well found a man of compassion and droll humor. Ulbrickson was a large young man with a strong voice, a commanding presence, an awesome work ethic and a dedication to rowing perfection. In time, he would become his own legend in Washington's rowing tradition.

The Huskies did not sweep the Hudson again for years. Victories came harder. Pocock's teachings had spread, via his coaching disciples, throughout American rowing. Ky Ebright developed California as a major force. The regattas between the Huskies and the Golden Bears drew huge crowds on Lake Washington.

Ebright's California crew of 1932 won the Olympics. The Ulbrickson crews were always up there-second, third, second, second again, third and second, through the years. Came the Depression and Seattle held public fund drives to send the crews east to Poughkeepsie.

In those hard times, people gave a dime, a quarter, maybe fifty cents, to showcase Seattle's most famous athletes.

Then, in 1936, Ulbrickson put together one of the all-time great crews in American rowing history. This was an eight stroked by Don Hume, a smooth, powerful oar. Hume was not big, but he was strong, and he had the beautiful rhythm needed in a stroke oar. Others on the crew were Joe Rantz, George Hunt and Jim McMillan (who would soon become the coach at the Massachusetts Institute of Technology), John White, Gordon Adam, Charles Day, Roger Morris, and the captain, Walter Bates. The coxswain was Robert Moch, who later became a coach at Yale.

This group did not start well. In the spring of 1936 the boat was sluggish and Ulbrickson was frustrated.

One practice day the coach saw George Pocock single-sculling in the distance. He brought his shell to a halt, waved his arms and beckoned Pocock. "George," said Ulbrickson, when Pocock drew alongside, "tell them what I am trying to teach them. Tell them what we try to accomplish around here."

Pocock circled the inert crew in his single scull. He spoke softly to them. George had a near-poetic gift for persuasion. He moved to each side of the shell as it rode lifeless in the waters of Windermere Bay. When he had finished speaking, George waved at Ulbrickson and rowed away.

Only those who have been up close to an eight oared shell can fully understand its astounding energy. The thin craft, weighing only 285 pounds, floats human power that weighs some 1,500 pounds. When oars cut into the water, in a single, controlled surge, eight pulling in unison, there is almost an explosion.

This is what happened on Windermere Bay in 1936. The crew Pocock had spoken to went on to beat everything that came in its way.

In April, it beat California by three lengths on Lake Washington, setting a course record.

On June 22 at Poughkeepsie, it broke last from the starting line but overhauled every boat in the race, pulled away from the field and won the national title handily.

In July, at the Olympic trials on Lake Carnegie, Washington finished well ahead of an outstanding Pennsylvania crew and, against a head wind, set an American record for 2,000 meters.

In August, in their preliminary Olympics race at Grunau, Germany, the Huskies rowed the 2,000 meters in six minutes and eight-tenths of a second-a world record.

When 120,000 Germans gathered in the Olympic stadium for the opening ceremonies, all athletes marched past Chancellor Adolph Hitler, who stood on the reviewing stand. It was a scene of military splendor. Among the German officers wearing great clusters of medals was Hermann Goering, he of the great Nordic belly.

Each of the crews from other nations lowered their country's flag as they marched, instep, past the reviewing stand. The kids from Seattle refused. They walked at their own paces, and they would not lower their flag in front of all this Nazi display.

The Olympics finals almost ended in disaster. Moch, the coxswain, could not hear the oral starting signal and the Huskies broke last, far behind. But this was a crew that "rowed with abandon, beautifully timed," as Pocock later said.

As they fell far behind, stroke Don Hume raised the beat, and Washington's new shell, the Husky Clipper, began to move. The Husky crew passed boat after boat, country after country, until, at last, there were only Germany and Italy left in front.

Germany and Italy. The huge crowd in the grandstand timed its chant with the German crew's stroke: "Deutsch-land! Deutsch-land! Deutsch-land!" Down on the water with one hundred meters to go in all this Teutonic bedlam, the voice of Robert Moch could not be heard two seats down the shell. He leaned forward so that the frail paper megaphone, strapped to his head, was almost in Hume's face.

"Gimme ten hard ones!" he screamed. Hume, who had been ill the night before, was scarcely conscious. But Moch's voice got through and Hume came to life. Moch beat the boat on both sides with his spruce blocks on the tiller lines. The vibration could be felt, setting the beat of a timed oar by each of the crewmen ... stroke! ... stroke! ... stroke!

"Ten hard ones!" he shouted, and the crew went out and beyond themselves. The Husky Clipper passed Germany, then Italy, and it was all over.

They were champions of the world.

How long ago?

Fifty-six years.

They are old men now, this Husky crew. Two are gone. Dr. Charles Day, the No. 2 oar, passed away a few years ago, and only last year Gordon Adam, the No. 6 oar, died at the age of 70. Members of this famous boat have a reunion every year. For their 40th anniversary, when they went out along Webster Point for a celebratory row, Al Ulbrickson pulled an oar in the No. 2 seat once occupied by Dr. Day.

After the Olympics came more victories as the Dour Dane turned out splendid crews. They won at Poughkeepsie in 1940 and 1941. These boats included a fine coxswain, Vic Forno, stroke Ted Garhart, and strong, well-timed oars pulled by the likes of Doyle Fowler, Tom Taylor, Walt Wallace, Chuck Jackson, and long-legged Johnny Bracken. Jackson would go on to coach at MIT.

The early '50s produced more fine Washington crews, but after that everything was in a decline.

The country had changed, and Seattle had changed with it. People became enamored of speed and noise. They turned out in great throngs to watch the belching, roaring hydroplanes, powered not by human strength and skill but by super-charged Rolls Royce and Allison airplane engines, boats that reached speeds of 200 miles per hour and more, boats that trailed huge swaths of white water called "roostertails."

The new heroes were the men of engines and daredevil driving: Stanley Sayres, Lou Fageol, Ted Jones, Bill Muncey, Wild Bill Cantrell. They became the waterside folk heroes of Seattle.

The boats had names like *Slo-Mo-Shun*, *Miss Seattle*, *Tempo* and *My Sweetie*. But even this would change, and the power boats took on blatantly commercial names like *Atlas Van Lines* and *Miss Pepsi*.

Now, if one were to walk among these huge crowds on August race days and ask people, "What was the Husky Clipper?" or "Who was George Pocock?" they would think he was addled.

Who could blame them? Generations have gone by, and there are new heroes, new celebrities.

Ulbrickson's last year as coach of the Washington oarsmen came in 1958, when the Huskies rowed at Henley, the place George Pocock had come from. This time the magic failed, and the Huskies were beaten.

But when the crews arrived in England, the kids found that each of their oars was wrapped in paper with the same penciled message from Pocock:

"Rowing a race is an art, not a frantic scramble. It must be rowed with head power as well as muscle power. From the first stroke all thoughts of the other crew must be blocked out. Your thoughts must be directed to you and your own boat, always positively, never negatively. Row your optimum power every stroke, try and increase the optimum.

"Men as fit as you, when your everyday strength is gone, can draw on a mysterious reservoir of power far greater. Then it is you can reach for the stars. That is the only way champions are made. That is the legacy rowing can leave you. Don't miss it."

The Huskies went on to Moscow, where they beat an outstanding Russian crew from the Trud Club. It would be the Dour Dane's last hurrah. Upon his return to Seattle Al Ulbrickson packed it in; he quit coaching forever and lived in retirement until he died in 1980.

George Pocock continued working in his shop, which was moved from the old Husky shell house to new quarters on Lake Union in 1964. His son, Stan, became a master boat builder in his own right and inherited his father's gift for coaching. He taught the Washington lightweight crews, then coached the freshman eights under Al Ulbrickson.

At one point every eight represented at Poughkeepsie used a Pocock shell—all 30 of them. In their years at the old Husky shell house at the Montlake Cut, George Pocock and his son turned out more than 1,000 handcrafted racing boats-eights, fours, pairs and singles.

George Pocock became a veritable Dalai Lama of boat racing. The man whose formal education ended at the age of 14 lectured at schools and rowing clubs all over the world until he died in 1976.

Something else went out of rowing then. Beautiful red cedar of the Northwest began to disappear; it became hard, then impossible to obtain. Stan Pocock was forced to use fiberglass and then Kevlar, a Dupont product. He sold the boat shop to Bill Tytus, a former Washington oarsman, who went on building shells in Everett. On every shell that goes out of the Everett shop there is the stamped famous signature: "Built by George Pocock Racing Shells, Inc."

And what of Charley McIntyre?

The young man who was first enthralled by George Pocock on the Montlake Cut in 1949 is now seventy years old.

There is still a bit of the Philadelphia street kid in him. But there is also a strong streak of Hiram Conibear. Like that early messiah of Washington rowing, Charley is an urger, a propagandist; he proselytizes, he promotes, and, like Hiram Conibear, he is obsessed with rowing as the true, the great, the only worthwhile sporting endeavor.

Charley spends almost every day teaching Seattle boys and girls to row in the Pocock tradition. He teaches out of the Seattle Tennis Club on Lake Washington and at Green Lake and Lake Union.

Everything must be Pocock: strong, well-timed, in a sport of feel and rhythm; each stroke must be perfect, nothing brutish about it, always silken smooth, or Charley will yell, "You're chopping wood, goddammit, you're chopping wood!"

Men who are messiahs never get enough. In 1988, Charley began calling up old oarsmen. He assembled a crew of old-timers: Guy Harper of Washington, '54, who himself joined the crusade; Bruce Bradley, who had rowed at Princeton; Art Wright, Naval Academy; Dave Haworth, Cornell; Roger Seeman, Wisconsin; John Aberle, Vesper Boat Club. The list grew. Soon they had several boatloads of men in their 50s and 60s and even 70s. They were teachers, surgeons, investment counselors, property managers, construction contractors.

They would row, they vowed, in the tradition of George Pocock. They called themselves the Ancient Mariners. They are coached by Charley McIntyre and Stan Pocock.

They are still rowing, these older men, these classic stylists, to preserve a great tradition.

They practice on Lake Union three times a week at 5:30 in the morning. Lake Union is good because, in the dead of winter, in the darkness, there are lights reflecting on the water to see by.

More visibility comes from the lights reflecting off Seattle's tall buildings—the buildings that rose and replaced the trees, just as Hiram Conibear said it would happen.

"New and bigger buildings will come," Connie told George Pocock. "See that water, all that water …. Someday there will be great tall buildings. What a city! What a place! You must come here!"

8

Good Enough for Any World

In everything that can be called art there is a quality of redemption. It may be pure tragedy, if it is high tragedy, and it may be pity and irony, and it may be the raucous laughter of the strong man. But down these mean streets, a man must go who is not himself mean, who is neither tarnished nor afraid .... He is the hero; he is everything. He must be a complete man and a common man and yet an unusual man. He must be, to use a rather weathered phrase, a man of honor—by instinct, by inevitability, without thought of it, and certainly without saying it. He must be the best man in his world and a good enough man for any world.

The paragraph above was written by Raymond Chandler to describe his fictional folk hero, Philip Marlowe. I once knew such a man as Chandler describes. He was a man of honor, a man of humility, a man of pride, a man of ideals and compassion; he was an unusual man, who lived at a time in Seattle when there was violence, and he was a genuine hero at a time when Seattle needed heroes badly because Seattle had much to be ashamed about. He had a fine mind, he read widely, but he did not wear his erudition, or his bravery, on his sleeve. His whole life was a work of art and at its end, thanks be to God and this man's strength, there was redemption.

Terry Pettus lived alone in a small houseboat at 2035 Fairview East.

He enjoyed company, and much of his laughter was joyous, even raucous. Terry had an instinctive, compassionate understanding of the human condition, and it was no fault of his that the world was not a more perfect place. He was drawn, helplessly, to his mission of trying to make the world better than it will ever be.

We would sit together until the tall morning hours and talk of many things—of cops and politicians, of brutality, of poetry, of literature, and of how nice it would be if we ever gave democracy a chance, if we really tried to make it work.

I would come to his houseboat and bring along a bottle of good Scotch, because I was working, and he was not. He lived in low-income retirement. Sometimes we would sip Johnny Walker Black Label, or if I had sold a story to some magazine, it would be Pinch Bottle. The quality of the liquor honored the elegance of the man.

In his houseboat Terry had a small wood stove that, along with the Scotch, drove away the winter dampness. Terry's place was lined with books, many of them obscure, books on the natural sciences or economics, dating back to another century. On his wall there was a portrait of his wife, Berta, who died in 1970, a haunting painting of a beautiful lady. It was one of the few portraits ever done by Terry's friend Kenneth Callahan.

"Oh, Lordy!" Terry would cry, when something interesting occurred to him. One night he talked about the now-defunct Seattle magazine called *The Town Crier*. He said it dealt with the arts, with amusements, that it was sometimes satirical, "sort of like the *New Yorker*." For a while, he said, he wrote for it under the name of Burris Hanley.

"I wrote a series called 'As I Remember.' " Terry said. "And I would write these little things, vignettes, you might call them. They were about 500 words and Ken Callahan would do the caricatures for them.

"One I wrote was about Jim Stevens. Now, Jim, you know was probably the most prolific writer we ever had in the Northwest. He wrote a dozen books and hundreds of magazine stories. Hell, he wrote for H. L. Mencken in the *American Mercury*. Jim wrote many of the Paul Bunyan stories, the great fables of the Northwest. It was Paul Bunyan, the giant logger, and Babe the Big Blue Ox. I knew Jim very well. He loved to sit around, get half full of moonshine, and he would sing these gospel songs, with the Cross of Jesus and everything else in them. And he created a few old ballads. I will never forget one he wrote. It went like this: 'Little birdie, little birdie, won't you sing me a song/ I've got such a short time to be here and a long time to be gone.' Oh, Lordy, he was talented!

That was the way Terry talked as we sat up far into the night.

"Berta and I," he said, "lived downtown in the Normandy Apartments. It's gone now, wiped out by the downtown freeway. I worked at the *Seattle Star* then, and the Normandy Apartments were only a couple of blocks away.

"One of my favorite places then was Doc Hamilton's. He had a place up near the Broadway district. The food was terrific. Doc was trained in New Orleans in the tradition of that type of cooking, and oh, Lordy, he would make a big production out of ham. When he got around to carving it, everyone would stand by, in a circle, like it was a ritual. He also served the best gin fizzes a man could hope for.

"Downstairs he had a high-rolling craps game, which maybe led to his downfall. Doc had a terrific interest in food. He could read and write, all right, but he never went to bookstores. Maybe it was because he was black, but he was not used to bookstores. So, I would buy cookbooks for him, and Doc was fascinated by the idea of anybody actually writing—books, for God's sake!—about food.

"Well, the way it was, Doc wanted to buy a house out in the Mount Baker district, a little outside his turf, and this raised a terrible stink. All the nicer people, the so-called nicer people, like politicians and judges, came to eat and drink at Doc's. He was paying off the pols and the cops, all right, but when he wanted to buy this house in Mount Baker that was too much. Doc tried to buy the house through another party, so they nailed him. They got him on gambling and the Prohibition laws, so Doc went over—he did some time in Walla Walla. It was a dirty goddamned shame. Doc died shortly after he got out of Walla Walla. He was a helluva nice and interesting man."

Terry worked at the *Star* and later at the *Tacoma Daily Ledger*. He could review plays and musicals and he could also go out on the streets and cover hard news.

Down these mean streets a man must go who is not himself mean ….

Terry saw it all. It was during the lumber strikes and dock strikes of the 1930s. It was a time when soldiers and the National Guard and the city cops were clubbing, tear-gassing, even shooting American workers who dared to form unions. This was not racism as we knew it in the 1960s, or as we know it today; this was true class warfare, and the streets of Tacoma and the streets of Seattle, particularly Railroad Avenue along the waterfront, became terribly mean. White laboring people were looked down upon as an inferior class.

If you were a cop or in the militia you were ordered to club your fellow citizens in order to open up picket lines and break strikes. Terry was in the middle of all this. Sometimes he could even speak wryly about it: "I always succeeded in getting on the wrong side of the lines when they were throwing tear gas. I used to chalk up six or seven tear gas episodes a day. The police would throw'em and the workers would pick them up and throw them back. So, it was a kind of grotesque Ping-Pong game."

Terry was in the middle of these battles and they shaped his life, partly because they happened during the Depression. At least he had a job then. But he watched as people, once prosperous people, walked the streets hungry. Hundreds would line up in hopes of getting a day's work. They poked into garbage cans for food, went to jail for stealing to feed their families. Some lived in shacks, tiny dwellings thrown together from scrap lumber and sheet metal. They called it Hooverville, a little self-governing community of the dispossessed along Railroad Avenue.

Berta and Terry lived well. They dined at the Italian Village on Fifth Avenue, or at Manca's, at Second and Marion, where they would feast on Manca's specialty, custardy pancakes called Dutch Babies. They ate at the Bohemia, up on Sixth Avenue, and the American Oyster House on Westlake. But the suffering of others was tearing Terry apart. His conscience was unrelenting. He saw men dressed in business suits, because they didn't own work clothes, shoveling mud, trying to earn money from some paltry public make-work program in Tacoma.

The big *Post-Intelligencer* newspaper strike came in 1936. The issue was whether Seattle and Tacoma newspaper employees could form a union. Terry became the first president of that union, the Pacific Northwest Newspaper Guild. This was a strike without violence. The picket line was manned by such people as tiny Abe Cohen, of the *P-I* copy desk, and skinny, frail Mike Donohoe, of the sports department. It seemed that such as these would be no match for the strike-breaking goons brought in by William Randolph (The Real) Hearst, who owned the paper. Hearst was the kind of power who could brag about starting the Spanish-American War. Strike? He had broken strikes before.

"Oh, Lardy," Terry laughed. The Scotch was good, and the fire in his small houseboat was warm as Terry continued. "We didn't know it then, but the labor movement in this town was just dying to take a crack at Hearst. He was everybody's favorite enemy. That first morning of the strike there were 22 Guild people on the picket line, not much muscle. But here they came! An army of longshoremen off the waterfront, tough men with longshoring hooks in their pockets. A few minutes later, here came the Teamsters. Dave Beck approved the strike! Then out came the teachers' union from the University of Washington.

"By midmorning, that wasn't a picket line! That was one living mass of people around that ratty old Hearst building at Sixth and Pine. People said the mayor, Johnny Dore, was in Dave Beck's hip pocket. I guess that was true. In any case, the Seattle cops were nice to us. I even saw one them show a lady picket how she should carry her sign. Hearst threatened to take the P-1 out of Seattle. So, Mayor Johnny Dore, who was elected with labor's support, got up there and said things like, 'Sooo, you're going to leave Seattle, Mr. Hearst! Then go away, Mr. Hearst. We don't want your kind corrupting our city and trying to destroy this great labor movement.' Oh, Lardy, he could turn it on. It was really something."

Hearst stayed. After 91 days he surrendered, and the Pacific Northwest Newspaper Guild became part of the community.

> *He must be a complete man and a common man and*
> *yet an unusual man ....*

Terry Pettus began to believe (as he put it) that the system was horseshit. The strikes, the tear gas, the indignities laid upon people, the hunger, the broken spirits .... he became more outraged by the Depression and what it did to people. He became more radical and this, perhaps, was inevitable. Terry grew up in Terre Haute, Indiana, where his father was a Protestant minister. He never heard anything about a vengeful God because his father was a Christian Socialist. The famous socialist Eugene V. Debs lived in Terre Haute, and Debs was so popular that when he ran for president, Terry's Boy Scout troop passed out campaign literature.

As an intellectual in Seattle, Terry saw society as a system built on the exploitation of weaker people. "The only way it survived," he said one night, "was in the pouring out of blood, the pouring out of misery. Oppression of people. The crushing of people. I thought then, and I think now, there must be a better way for humankind to live."

Terry became less a journalist and more a man of action. When his paper, the *Tacoma Ledger*, discontinued publication, Terry worked as editor of the *Willapa Harbor Pilot*, where he and Berta led a successful local campaign for public ownership of electric power companies. Then Terry became active in the Washington Commonwealth Federation. Formed in 1935, the Federation was a political coalition of unions, farmers, some socialists, certainly some communists, quite a few teachers and a lot of idealists.

The Washington Commonwealth Federation proposed that the state take over shut-down factories and put people back to work. Its members believed that there was a new class of rights, among them the right to have a job. They organized, precinct after precinct; they began to use the Democratic Party to advance their ideas.

"So, all of a sudden," Terry said, "we overwhelmed conservatives in the 1936 state Democratic convention. In one fell swoop, for God's sake, we controlled the Democratic Party. It was OUR party. Through the next few years the Washington Commonwealth Federation began to get people elected. We helped elect Henry Jackson and Warren Magnuson to the U.S. House of Representatives."

Terry Pettus began to go deeper into politics. The Washington Commonwealth Federation began to come apart, split by rival unions and factions. But Terry now was committed. In 1938 he joined the Communist Party.

Soon he was editor of the radical *Washington New Dealer*. He made no attempt to hide his Communist membership. He exhorted people to become active in politics, to learn about issues; living and surviving in a capitalist democracy, he told them, was not a part-time endeavor.

So, he wrote and gave speeches and went to meetings. As the 1930s drew to a close, there was war in Europe. There had been the Spanish Civil War, of course, the warm-up for Nazi Germany and Fascist Italy. Many of Terry's friends joined the Lincoln Brigade and went over to fight for the Spanish Republic. Many never were heard from again. Right next door to Terry's houseboat was a man who had fought in the Lincoln Brigade. He came home from Spain to find he could not get a job because he was branded "a premature anti-fascist."

There were military dictatorships in Germany, Italy and Japan. Germany's Nazi blitzkrieg began to ravish Europe, and Joseph Stalin signed a non-aggression pact with Adolph Hitler. Many of Terry's friends in the Communist Party bailed out. But Terry stayed. "Many people I respected very much," Terry said, "left the Party. They were idealistic people who couldn't stand it when the Soviet Union would make such an agreement with that horrible monster we called Hitlerism and Nazism. I disagreed with that."

Terry was still active in the Washington Commonwealth Federation which became even more divided after the Nazi-Soviet pact. One Sunday morning in 1941 Terry was giving a speech at a Federation meeting. A man came up to the podium and handed him a message.

"I looked at the message and then I looked at the audience," Terry said. "Then I said, 'This has just come in. I'm not sure where it came from, but here it is. The Japanese have bombed Pearl Harbor.'

"I am looking at those people out there and to this day I can't describe what really happened in that audience. I tried to say something … what could you say? There seemed to be a great gasp that engulfed the whole room. Some of the people began to cry and some of them began to pray. My goddamn little speech was over."

The Depression disappeared. The Commonwealth Federation got into the war effort—scrap drives, volunteer work, defense jobs. Many of its members joined the army. Terry went down to his draft board and demanded to be drafted. "They said I couldn't be drafted because I was editor of a paper and so I was essential to a war industry. A war industry! A few years later I was being charged and sentenced to prison for being editor of that paper!"

The *New Dealer* was renamed the *New World*. Pettus wrote editorials calling for an invasion of Europe, a second front to relieve pressure on the Soviet Union. (Non-aggression had not lasted long;

German troops were deep inside Russia.) Under Pettus, the *New World* campaigned against racial discrimination and for public services, including medical care and old-age pensions. It thundered against anti-Semitism. During all this time, while Terry edited and wrote, he also worked in the shipyards.

Terry continued to fight for progressive measures; he even ran for Congress. When the war finally ended in 1945, Terry Pettus, the idealist, thought that the future held promise. With fascism defeated, the world might become a better place. The Washington Commonwealth Federation dissolved. But Seattle became far different from what Terry had hoped. For Terry and his fellow radicals, it became a place of apprehension.

One night, in his houseboat, Terry talked about this. "In a way, the progressive, wonderful city that I knew had disappeared. I felt terribly uneasy. One day I picked up the phone and called my dad, the Christian Socialist minister. I felt disturbed, I couldn't escape the feeling that something was terribly wrong. I told my Dad, 'As you know, I am not a very religious person myself, but I want you to pray for us all.' "

The terrible time was not long in coming. It began with the FBI agents who shadowed Terry and Berta. The Pettuses' telephones were tapped. They got so used to the FBI agents that when the agents lost the trail, Terry and Berta would wait at the next street intersection and beckon them to come on.

In 1946, the Republicans swept into power. A man out of Spokane, Albert Canwell, was among those elected to the State Legislature. He became chairman of the Legislature's Joint Fact-Finding Committee on Un-American Activities. The communist witch hunt was on.

"First it attacked the University," Terry said. "Now, the University was the fountain, shall we say, of intellectual freedom. The faculty was terrorized. Three tenured professors were fired. The hearings went on and on, big headlines. They wanted names and more names—not just of communists but anybody liberal. Names got them more headlines. We were ahead of the times. The Canwell Committee carried on its witch hunt for more than a year, long before anybody heard of Joe McCarthy and McCarthyism."

It was a time of fear in Seattle and the nation. Sick fear. The radical right-wingers, the ultra-conservatives, trampled civil liberties, even civil debate and discussion.

"People were whipped up and emotional," Terry said. "If the law had permitted us to be executed, we probably would have been."

Terry Pettus, with seven others, was charged under the Smith Act with "conspiring to teach or advocate the overthrow of the government." They were not charged with actually "teaching" or "advocating" overthrow of the government, merely with "conspiring" to do so.

"The conspiracy charge is a difficult one to counter," Terry said. "It goes back to English common law, which says that he who imagines the king dead is guilty of treason."

Terry remembers taking the stand in federal court—it was his birthday, August 15, 1953. A week earlier, one of his co-defendants, William Pettit, had committed suicide. Terry knew what they would ask him. He knew what they wanted—names and more names. Who else attended your meetings? Who were the others in your union? Names. Terry and his colleagues would not answer. With the trial still in progress, Terry was found in contempt and sentenced to 73 days in jail. He lost 25 pounds.

One night at his houseboat, Terry recalled: "I told the court that I would answer any questions about myself or those on trial with me. But I would not name others. I would not add to the virus, the sickness, of our society by betraying other people."

At the end of an agonizing, six-month trial, Judge William Lindberg sentenced Terry and his co-defendants to three years in the federal penitentiary. Terry Pettus was stunned. He considered the sentence an affront to justice. The conviction was quickly overturned by the Ninth Circuit Court of Appeals. The Supreme Court later found that the Smith Act conspiracy convictions were unconstitutional.

Terry and Berta continued to live on their houseboat. They had bought it for $1,000 in the early days of the war. The moorage fee was $6 a month. Terry was free, yes, but he was a pariah. It was still the McCarthy era. Old acquaintances would cross the street to avoid talking to him. Friends were afraid to be seen in his company. There was no hope of getting a job on any newspaper in any city in the state of Washington. This most gifted of men, who could cover street stories, murders, trials, who could review plays and musicals, who could write satire, human-interest stories, this all-purpose man of letters was shut off from making a living in the craft he loved. He was forced to write pulp-magazine detective stories to bring in just a little income.

Terry didn't talk much about these times. When I asked him why he didn't write a book, he said the memories were too painful. Sometimes, as we sat up and talked, I would think about a passage in the play *Inherit the Wind*. It was a play about the Scopes "monkey trial" in Dayton, Tennessee in 1925. The young defendant, Bertram Cates, jailed for teaching evolution in a fundamentalist community, is being defended by Clarence Darrow. The great trial lawyer had defended men like Terry Pettus, outcasts in their own communities. So, in the play, when it appeared that the easiest thing for the young man to do was recant, to say he was sorry, that he'd made a mistake, Darrow says:

"I understand what Bert is going through. It's the loneliest feeling in the world—to find yourself standing up when everybody else is sitting down. To have everybody look at you and say, 'What's the matter with him?' I know. I know what it feels like. Walking down an empty street, listening to the sound of your own footsteps. Shutters closed, blinds drawn, doors locked against you. And you aren't sure whether you're walking toward something—or just walking away."

How easy it would have been for Terry. Doors would have opened to him, old friends would smile their greetings .... all he had to do was say, "I'm sorry, I made a mistake." All he had to do was go before these ... these creatures, these headline-hunting fearmongers and say, "I will tell you anything you want to know. Names? You want names? Here, I've got some names for you. I'm sorry, I made a mistake."

But Terry was not that kind of man. In the evenings, over Scotch, he would sometimes roar his defiance. "Me apologize? Apologize for what? I worked for pensions, medical care, good working conditions, decent housing, security. Would they expect me to apologize for THAT?"

He must be a complete man. He must be, to use a rather weathered phrase, a man of honor-by instinct, by inevitability, without thought of it, and certainly without saying it.

The years went by. Terry and Berta continued to live on the

houseboat at 2035 Fairview East. They were lonely years, but they became less lonely as they made new friends. Still, times were hard, and Terry and Berta were not welcome in many places; Terry had become a non-person in Seattle. One day the phone rang. The caller said he worked for the United States government. He said he did not want to come to the houseboat. Could they meet in a park, in the evening, after dark?

When they met, the man from the government began to describe the nature of his visit.

"I know a man back in Washington. He says he can't come out in the open with you. My guy is a politician and he says he would be ruined if he got mixed up with you. Here ..."

He handed Terry a large wad of cash.

"My guy says he has an idea of what you're going through. He says he knows that you helped him get elected. He wants you to have this money."

Terry smiled thinly as he told the story. I said to Terry, "It was ..."

"Yes, it was Warren G. Magnuson," Terry said, "but you cannot use this story until Maggie is gone."

There is a saying, coined by my friend Ralph Geele: "Time heals all wounds. Sooner or later, your enemies, or theirs, drop dead."

Many of Terry's old enemies disappeared or died or became obsolete in retirement. Berta died in 1971, leaving Terry even more alone. But now it was different. Because of his warmth and humor and enthusiasm, his genuine love for people, new friends began to seek him out. They were younger men and women, many of whom were his neighbors in the houseboat community. They were too young to know about the witch hunts and, indeed, times had changed, and they were not shocked when Terry told them that he had once been an outcast, a Communist.

He began to see more and more people. During this later period of his life, when I knew him, he would go to Susan Gerrard's home on Queen Anne Hill for dinner. Susan had two bright young daughters, who were enchanted by Terry. He had a way of riveting the attention of younger people. Susan's older daughter, Jessica, wrote an honors history paper on Terry for her class at Mount Holyoke College. Beth, the younger girl, sat transfixed as Terry told her about the timber and waterfront strikes; he was a man who did not make history seem dull.

In the early 1960s, Terry almost single-handedly saved Seattle's houseboats. The houseboats were considered doomed because they discharged raw sewage into Lake Union. There were eviction notices and nobody except the houseboat people seemed to care. Terry, the old radical, went among his neighbors on the water and exhorted them to fight back. He formed the Floating Homes Association.

Terry stalked City Hall, sitting in on committee meetings, accumulating the ammunition he needed as the administrative secretary and newsletter editor of the Floating Homes Association.

"Sure," he would say, "we dropped sewage into the lake, but the city itself was discharging stuff-from 13 raw sewage outfalls. People said, 'You can't plumb a houseboat.' But this—he pointed to the floor—is the first houseboat they plumbed.

"We stuck together. The City Council passed an L.I.D. (Local Improvement District) and let us build sewers. We saved the houseboats and cleaned up the lake."

In the spring of 1982, younger people began to understand, to appreciate, the precious resource Seattle had in Terry Pettus. A talented young producer, John DeGraf, put together a splendid television documentary on Terry's life and times. Then, wonder of wonders, the mayor of Seattle, Charles Royer, honored the old battler by proclaiming March 7, 1982, "Terry Pettus Day." Terry was a beloved citizen in a community that once shunned him.

Terry Pettus died on October 7, 1984. He lived to be 80 years old. His life was very nearly a work of art and he lived to witness his own redemption.

He was the best man in his world and a good enough man for any world.

9

Jew Mike

Hiram Conibear, the father of Washington rowing, had his vision in 1912. He saw great tall buildings replacing the great tall trees of Seattle. Viewed from this distance, 80 years later, it doesn't seem like a good trade-off. Tall buildings are the stuff of contractors and developers; grouped together in one small downtown area they can be brutal and intimidating.

Steel, glass, aluminum, brick and marble, braced together and rising toward the clouds, can have a certain majesty. From a distance they are impressive, tall pillars signifying that indefinable something we call progress. But there is a penalty to be paid for this alleged grandeur.

Each of these great structures exists on its own terms. Not our terms, human terms, but the terms of the building itself-a cruel giantism that dominates and bullies whatever is below. Every time a Columbia Center goes up, a price must be paid on the sidewalk. When a Sheraton Hotel destroys a whole block, something real is lost. Union Squares One and Two exact a similar forfeiture of human spirit. We become ants.

A stroll in Seattle's downtown used to be fun. It was low-rise and low-rent: a pawnshop here, a tailor there; a pool hall, small and cheap cafes, a music store, places to get your shoes fixed, barbershops, weathered cafeterias. It was all these and more, part of a street life that belonged to all of us.

I am thinking especially about Union Street. It was where I spent much of my young adult life. Union Street, the busy part of it from Fourth Avenue on up to Ninth, could provide one with a baccalaureate in street smarts; it was a trade school of interpersonal values, a cement campus of camaraderie.

Union Street was a cluster of small hotels-the Windsor, the Caledonia, the Navarre, the Ambassador, the Wilhard. People lived in those places and came out to be part of life on the street.

"It was different then, it was safe," George Chemeres, the fight manager, tells you. George was one of the hundreds of night people who lived and thrived around Union Street. As a boy he worked at the Quality Food Market, which stayed open 24 hours a day.

"Guys could gamble and walk around with huge wads of cash," George says. "Today if you tried that you'd get rolled, get your head knocked off."

The old Union Street is gone now, obliterated by the Sheraton Hotel and its parking lot; by the Convention Center, by the two Union Square buildings.

The Magic Inn was at the comer of 6th and Union, a basement nightclub. Vic Naon ran it. His hostess for many years was Dottie Venable, who knew everybody on Union Street. Holly Winters, a cute young tap dancer and singer, got her start there. The Magic Inn booked top night-club acts—a young Sammy Davis, Jr., entertained at the Magic Inn with the Will Mastin Trio.

Next door to the Magic Inn was Al Phillips Cleaners and above that was, so help me, a netted golf driving range. Next to that was an elegant pool hall where you could go and watch world class talent compete for money.

I worked for the *Seattle Star* back in 1944. A half block down from the *Star* was the Richelieu Cafe, a hangout for newspaper people, ball players, fighters and politicians. Dick Sharp, the great boxing writer, would come in late, after he put the P-1 to bed. He would labor his 300 pounds over to the Richelieu, where he held court in one of its large booths.

One of the Richelieu regulars was a politician known officially as Progressive Jack Taylor. He had his name legally changed to Progressive Jack Taylor because he so frequently ran for office. Directly across the street was the Eagles Auditorium, a part of which housed the Washington State Press Club. There I learned to drink whiskey sours. Once, oh, exalted moment, I heard the great Paul Robeson give a talk on democracy, followed by a short, beautiful ballad he sang with no accompaniment. He simply cupped one hand to his ear and every note was true.

I covered night baseball games then, and on a couple of occasions I brought Casey Stengel into the Italian Club. Customers entered mid-block, between Sixth and Seventh, and then climbed one long flight of stairs. Stengel managed Oakland. One year later, 1948, he managed the New York Yankees to his first of many world championships. Casey loved to drink and stay up late; he had a head like an oaken bucket.

The Italian Club, like the Richelieu, was a hangout for politicians, ballplayers and newspaper people. In the 1930s it had slot machines along the barroom wall. The Italian Club was run by Johnny Scali and Louie Rispoli, and the food was always outstanding. Most of the Coast League ball players of that day used the Italian Club as an after-game watering hole: Jo-Jo White, Bill Lawrence, Joe Orengo, Lefty O'Doul, Bill Ramsey, Babe Herman and many more.

The beat cops on Union Street were John Foley and Bob Dodge, but they were only part of what made the street safe. It was the people: safety in numbers, knowing each other, each to his own business, each to his own way.

Below the Italian Club was Bob's Chili Parlor, a raffish place of almost Runyonesque flavor. Bob's Chili was owned by Bob Kevo, Al Benson and Harry Naon. It was a hangout for boxers and lawyers. Chemeres always brought his fighters around, showcasing them before a big card, and so, for that matter, did Jack Hurley, another famous fight manager of that day. Chemeres brought in such fighters as Hobo Wiler, Larry Buck, Charley Reno and, on a higher national level, such heavyweight brawlers as Jerry Quarry and George Foreman. Chemeres and Hurley sold thousands of fight tickets out of Bob's Chili.

Gambling? There was plenty of that. Poker games and crapgames used to float around Union Street. There was a legendary character whose home was Union Street and Pike Street between Sixth and Eighth. At Sixth and Pike there used to be a two-story building on the corner. It once housed a jewelry store, then later one of those sports shops that sell "authorized" shirts and jackets with "official" National Football League and major-league baseball logos on them.

This was where Jew Mike had his gambling upstairs.

Sixth and Pike was the epicenter of Jew Mike's legendary games, although, since games moved, he might be found on Union Street. He worked Sixth and Pike and across the street where the Sheraton Hotel now stands. Later, and more permanently, Jew Mike operated at the old Navarre Hotel, between Sixth and Seventh on Pike, in what he called the Rainbow Club.

Jew Mike.

"They don't make 'em like Jew Mike anymore," a friend who knew him well once told me. He would talk about Jew Mike only on condition that I wouldn't use his real name. We'll call him Charlie.

"I'm 73 now," Charlie said, "and I grew up there as a street kid. This was back in the 1930s and Jew Mike took a liking to me.

"He was a high roller, a big gambler. There were a lot of high rollers around then. A lot of it was local talent, but high rollers came in from Alaska, Montana and California. I got to be a high roller myself and Jew Mike liked that about me."

Jew Mike was not a term of opprobrium, bluntly anti-Semitic. Meyer "Jew Mike" Rothstein loved to be called that. It was Meyer Rothstein's nickname and he was proud of it. He would regularly send in donations to the *P-I* Christmas Fund when Frank Lynch was doing the "Howling 'Em Out" column, a not-so-subtle name-dropping operation to force people with money to give.

Meyer Rothstein would send in money and he would always sign his donation "J. Mike."

Jew Mike never gambled in his own joints. He had a reputation of being a "straight" guy, who ran honest games of 4-5-6, barbotte, lowball and craps. When Jew Mike gambled himself, he went to other places in town, and in those days of city administration "tolerance," there seemed to be hundreds of them.

These old street guys like my friend Charlie will tell you how Jew Mike once lost $70,000 on the turn of one card in lowball.

Think of that for a moment. $70,000. Those were Depression dollars. What would he lose on the turn of a card today?

So, Jew Mike ran "straight" games in the old Rainbow Club. Which meant that high rollers from other towns could come into Seattle, gamble big, and not get cheated.

"That's the way it used to be around Union Street and over on

Pike," Charlie said. "People gave their word and you could sleep on it. If you were kinky or wrong, they stayed away from you, you didn't belong in their circle.

"We all walked the street at night with lots of cash on us. Jew Mike always carried plenty of folding money, but he was safe. Today, they'd stick a shiv in you for ten bucks."

Like all high rollers, Jew Mike drank sparingly. An alcohol buzz is bad for the gambling profession. Jew Mike rolled his own Bull Durham cigarettes. He would tip a bar girl five dollars to light his cigarette.

They got him in 1946. Jew Mike pleaded guilty to one of three counts of income-tax evasion. All gamblers seem to run afoul of Uncle Fed. Jew Mike pleaded guilty to a charge that he paid a 1942 income tax of $30,233.94 on an income of $56,236.98. The feds proved he owed $111,640.56 on a true income of $155,294.90.

U.S. District Judge Charles Leavy, in Tacoma, sentenced Meyer Rothstein to nine months at McNeil Island, but he ended up serving his time in the county jail. Frank Lynch went down to the county jail to see Jew Mike. He found him to be ailing and lonely. In his column, Lynch explained why Jew Mike requested transfer to McNeil.

"The island is not the grim place it looks," Lynch wrote. "The salty breeze blows into the cell blocks. There are gardens, vegetables and flowers to putter about in. There is work and golden sunshine."

Jew Mike, the legend among Union Street regulars, died on September 15, 1962. His obituary in the *Seattle Times* was two inches long. Legends do not last much beyond their generation.

He was a high roller, Jew Mike. But he was not alone among Seattle gamblers. At about the time Jew Mike ran afoul of the feds, another and very different kind of gambler was on his way. While Jew Mike could win or lose $70,000 on the turn of a card, the result had no impact on any part of Seattle. This other gambler changed the city, changed the world, and he, too, is half forgotten by the young people of today's sophisticated, metropolitan city.

10

The Men Who Shrunk the World

There were few things William Allen would have in common with Jew Mike, the celebrated high roller of Union Street. They were of different planets. Jew Mike lived in hotel rooms and roamed the streets. Allen, impeccably tailored, lived in the exclusive Highlands; he orbited in a corporate world beyond the imagination of any street person. Yet Allen truly did have one thing in common with Jew Mike—he would roll the dice, bet the wad, go for the main chance; he would wager the company on his own judgment and that of the men who worked for him.

Bill Allen ruled The Boeing Airplane Company from 1945 until his retirement in 1968. He was a lawyer. He thought in linear, logical terms. Before he became Boeing's president he had handled the company's legal affairs for 20 years, and he was an expert in aviation law. But he knew almost nothing about manufacturing airplanes and very little about finance. So, when the board of directors asked Bill Allen to head up Boeing in 1944, he put them off.

"I'm not the man you want," he said, in effect. "There are better men than me to run this company."

He even confided to his wife that he was not competent to handle the job.

But the company directors persisted. Allen kept saying no. "Look around, find someone else. I don't want the job. I'll try to help you find somebody."

But he finally acceded. On September 1, 1945, Allen became the fifth president in The Boeing Company's history. Allen would need all the luck he could find.

On the day he took over the company, the Air Force canceled a B-29 bomber contract. More cancellations followed. World War II was over. Allen had to reduce Boeing's Seattle payroll from 35,000 to 6,000. Airplane sales, which were $421 million in 1945, dropped to only $13 million during Allen's first year as president.

In the lexicon of Jew Mike, he was about tapped out.

The story is told about the young staffer who told Bill Allen that he, the boss, didn't understand some contract proposal "because you started at the top, not at the bottom."

This amused Allen. "I'll have you know," he said, "that when I started it was ALL bottom."

When he took over Allen was surrounded by talented young engineers, some still in their 20s. Some had worked on the B-17 and B-29 bomber programs and later on the piston-driven Stratocruiser.

They were men like Maynard Pennell, a designer who once had worked for Douglas on the famed DC-3 transport. There were others: Ed Wells, Joe Sutter, Bob Withington, Lynn Olason, George Martin, Jim Wright, Reg Watney, Milt Heineman, Bill Cook, Dick Rouzie, Lloyd Goodmanson and Harlowe Longfelder. There was also the legendary workaholic, Jack Steiner.

Let any one of these leave a room and you would have a brain drain.

A surprising number of them came from the University of Washington, where they had studied under Professor Frederick K. Kirsten, a famed pioneer in aviation research and head of the school's aeronautical engineering department.

These men talked the ratified technical language of engineering and science; at times Bill Allen must have thought he was listening to Swahili.

But Allen, the lawyer, spoke plain English. He mastered his engineers' technical jargon. At important meetings he would go around the table, listening to each expert, making good use of his notebook. At the end—sometimes immediately—he made his decision. Allen had an almost inborn sense of command, and the phrase "Allen of Boeing" began to command respect in the sporty game of airliners and airplanes.

"The sporty game." Bill Allen, like the street gambler Jew Mike, was not afraid to take a chance.

About two months after Allen became president, a young Boeing engineer named George Schairer was in Germany—specifically, he was outside of Braunschweig, where Reichsmarschall Herman Goering once had his Aeronautical Research Institute. The victorious Allies were after all sorts of technical and scientific data there; Schairer was interested in anything that had to do with German flying capability.

One pile of records and documents riveted Schairer's attention. The papers revealed that the Germans were very much involved in swept-wing design of aircraft powered with jet engines.

Jack Steiner was a young engineer at Boeing, hired by Schairer. In fact, Schairer had put him on the Boeing payroll while Jack still was working on his master's degree at MIT.

Steiner doesn't remember the details of the seven-page letter Schairer had sent from Germany to Ben Cohn, an aerodynamicist at Boeing. "But what it added up to," Steiner recalls now, "was that we had better get our asses turned around and into swept wing."

Again, when Allen took office, Joe Sutter was a young aviation engineering officer for the Navy, based at Eniwetok in the South Pacific. Sutter got two letters on the same day. Each was a job offer, one from Douglas, the other from Boeing. Boeing offered him $206 a month; Douglas offered $216. He took the Douglas offer because, as Joe says today, "ten dollars was a lot of money."

As it happened, Joe, a 1943 University of Washington graduate in aeronautical engineering, left the Navy and returned to Seattle, where his wife was about to have a child. He didn't want to move to Southern California, at least not then. So, Joe took a "temporary" job at Boeing. He wrote to Douglas, explaining that they would hear from him later; Douglas sent a nice reply, telling Joe to "come when you can." Joe never went to Douglas. He stayed with Boeing for 41 years and still is a consultant on yet-to-be built airliners.

Steiner and Sutter became two of the big players at Boeing. Steiner was best known for his engineering and program management work on the 727; he later headed up the 737 and 747 programs. Sutter eventually became chief engineer on the building of the 747.

But both of them, while still in their 20s, were key figures in the design and management of the earlier 707, the jet transport that would revolutionize the world's air travel.

Looking back on the late 1940s and early 1950s, Jack Steiner thinks the two exceptional Boeing people were George Schairer and Ed Wells. George had an exceptional mind. I don't think Bill Allen trusted him all that much, because George had a way of projecting his thoughts that was disconcerting. I don't think Allen trusted me all that much, either.

"Wells was a quiet man with a controlled, careful mind. He had a great gift for storing material in his head and then making the right choice. There would be options to consider and Wells would make a choice. Two days later we'd wonder why we hadn't done that in the first place."

Following World War II, Boeing built and sold 56 Stratocruisers. This was Bill Allen's decision and it was a money-loser. But he wanted to keep his top employees and he wanted to establish Boeing in the commercial transport market. The Stratocruisers were the last propeller-powered airplanes Boeing ever built.

Swept-wing design came in 1946, just as George Schairer said it would. At Schairer's urging, Boeing built a new high-speed wind tunnel, capable of testing a swept-wing aircraft. The tunnel was designed and built under the direction of Bill Cook, assisted by Bob Withington. In his book *The Road to the 707*, Cook remarks drily that things were different then, that today "two relatively junior engineers would not be considered" in designing a wind tunnel.

What came out of this tunnel testing was the B-47 bomber, powered by six jet engines. It flew like a dream and set a transcontinental speed record, covering 2,289 miles in 3 hours and 46 minutes. But, more important, when Bill Allen rode in it, he realized immediately that all piston-powered commercial airliners soon would become obsolete.

They were a remarkable team of designers and technological specialists at Boeing in those formative post-World War II years. One Boeing engineer told me, "These were guys who could look at some numbers on paper and they could visualize exactly what the airplane should look like."

That is just what happened on Oct. 21, 1948, when a contingent of Boeing experts visited Wright Field in Ohio. The Air Force's chief of bomber development urged them to abandon a turboprop design and concentrate on building a bomber that would use Pratt and Whitney's new J57 turbojet engine, one with 10,000 pounds of thrust, almost three times more powerful than the engines used on the B-47. The Boeing group was composed of chief engineer Ed Wells and designers Schairer, Withington, Vaughn Blumenthal, Art Carlson and Maynard Pennell.

What followed was one of the most remarkable stories in aviation-design history. These Boeing engineers went back to their rooms at the Van Cleve Hotel in nearby Dayton. One of them went out to a hobby shop and bought some balsa wood, some glue and a couple of knives. For that entire weekend they stayed in their rooms and began designing an eight-jet giant of an airplane—one with the sleek, swept-back wings used on the B-47.

By Monday morning, they had 33 pages of designs prepared, complete with drawings and a balsa-wood model. The Air Force bought it. That was the B-52, a bomber in use to this day.

The B-47 and the B-52 were important, but to prosper as a company, Bill Allen believed, Boeing would have to get into the commercial jet market. The formal decision to take the big gamble came at a board of directors meeting on April 22, 1952.

The meeting began at 1 o'clock with 12 Boeing directors present. According to the minutes of that meeting, Allen "called in a panel consisting of Mr. Ralph Bell, assistant sales manager Mr. Maynard Pennell, chief of preliminary design; Mr. George Schairer, chief of technical staff and Mr. Lyle Wood, chief engineer.

"Each of these gentlemen presented certain aspects of the design of the Model 707, together with a comparison of the 707 to other known transports and how each would fit into the military and commercial requirements ...."

It was decided to build a prototype of the 707. Y. O. Yeasting, one of the directors, "stated that in his opinion such a prototype would cost between thirteen and a half and fifteen million dollars."

The 707 prototype eventually would cost sixteen million dollars, all of it Boeing funds. The sum amounted to one-quarter of the net worth of Boeing. Bill Allen had rolled the dice—he was betting the company.

Things happened very fast after that. A section of the Renton plant was walled off with plywood. Pennell was in charge of what came to be called the "skunk works," a term that many Boeing people think was borrowed from Lockheed; actually, its origin was found in the comic strip "L'il Abner," where the "skonk works" was a humorous fixture.

The 707, later designated the 367-80, finally became the Dash-80. It was a prototype, what company experts called a "one of," meaning one of a kind. Jack Steiner would refer to it as "a flying testbed," and it was built in the remarkably short time of 26 months by a surprisingly small number of people—300 designers, technicians and supervisors and about 300 shop workers.

And they did work. They worked almost around the clock, seven days a week, and Steiner's own devotion to the Dash-80 became legendary. "I could communicate," he says today, "and I could drive people. And the word got around—it's a hot job."

As Steiner tells it today, "I was what you'd call the point man." Which meant that politicians and VIPs had to see him first before they visited the Renton plant. He didn't want them slowing down the skunk works' schedule.

The Dash-80 rolled out of its Renton hangar at exactly 4 p.m. on May 14, 1954. It was the time of a working shift change, and some 8,000 people were on hand to see this brown-and-yellow beauty. They were all there: Bill Allen, his technical wizards, politicians, newsreel cameras, all the press, even William E. Boeing, the company founder. The Renton High School band played up a storm. There was a lot of cheering and gee-whizzing because the Dash-80, as everyone knew, was the swept-wing commercial carrier of Boeing's future.

Boeing had plenty of good test pilots to fly the Dash-80. These were guys like Lew Wallick, Brien Wygle, Jack Waddell, Sandy McMurray, Jim Gannett and Tom Layne—all of them with jet flying experience in the B- 47 and the B-52. You couldn't ask for better pilots.

But there was one pilot in particular, a rangy, drawling swashbuckler named A. M. "Tex" Johnston, who was going to fly the Dash-80 and make history with it. A swashbuckler—that's all this high-risk, go-for-broke, bet-the-company scenario needed.

Yes, the Dash-80 was insured. An outfit called the United States Aviation Underwriters Insurance Group agreed to cover the "one of," the new jet on the tarmac, for $15 million, the largest such aircraft insurance policy ever written. On one condition. The Dash-80 was insured as long as one man and one man alone was pilot in command— Mr. Alvin Melvin Johnston, who came out of Kansas and wore big hats and was called Tex because he wore cowboy boots.

There was good reason for that provision. Tex Johnston's jet experience went back to October 1944, when he was project pilot for the Bell XP-59A, the first jet-powered airplane ever built in the United States.

He was also the primary test pilot on the X-1, a bullet-shaped rocket ship that later would break the sound barrier with Chuck Yeager at the controls. Tex had flown the X-1 to Mach 0.99 and easily could have broken the sound barrier—except that the military reserved that right for itself.

Tex became chief test pilot at Bell Aircraft in 1946. He came to Boeing in 1948 as project pilot for the B-47. In 1952 he was project pilot for the eight-jet B-52. In 1953 he became chief of flight testing for Boeing.

Tex was far more than a daredevil jet jockey; he had a deep knowledge of engineering, engine performance and the subtleties of aerodynamics. He was the right man to fly Boeing's new prototype, which became nothing less than a flying gene pool for the generations of swept-wing jets to come.

There was trouble ahead for the Dash-80, but gambler Bill Allen's luck held.

A week after roll-out, Johnston was conducting high-speed taxiing tests. Completing a 90-degree turn, Tex felt the airplane heel to the left. What he saw out of the cockpit window was appalling—something called "the rear trunnion" attachment to the left landing gear had collapsed. Tex was looking at his number one engine resting on the ground; he also saw part of the landing gear protruding through the left wing.

It could have been worse. The trunnion might have collapsed on landing after the Dash-80's initial flight. As it turned out, the Dash-80 went into sick bay for two months; landing gear repaired, the plane was pronounced ready to fly on July 15, 1954.

As Tex remembered the big day in his book, *Jet Age Test Pilot*, the Renton airport and the surrounding hillsides were packed with people.

"The populace of the Seattle area was turning out to witness the maiden flight of Boeing's pride, its bid for the lead in the dawning jet age. The Dash-80, wearing new yellow and brown colors, gleamed in the sunlight on the south ramp adjacent to a flight-line hangar ...."

Joe Sutter, who headed the aerodynamics unit on the Dash-80, was in the crowd. "We were all thrilled by it," Joe said, "but we were nervous. When a plane is all new, you are worried that something could have dropped through the cracks."

Tex went over to Bill Allen and said, "This airplane is as good as we can make it. I'm ready to fly."

"Good luck," Allen said, and turned away. Allen, Tex thought, looked tired and stooped, the whole weight of the company on his shoulders.

Johnston and Dix Loesch, his copilot, began to taxi. The Renton Airport was closed to all other planes. The pilots went through an exhaustive checklist. As the plane picked up speed on Runway 33, Loesch called out the speed, 130 miles per hour, and the Dash-80 left the runway. Tex took it into a steep climb angle; now there was no doubt—the Dash-80 could climb like a home-sick angel.

When he brought it to landing at Boeing Field and taxied up to the hangar, they were all there—a welcome committee of designers and engineers: Ed Wells, George Schairer, Wellwood Beall, George Martin, Maynard Pennell, Bill Cook, Dick Rouzie, Joe Sutter—all of them, and many more, who had created this entirely new and revolutionary prototype of a jet transport.

"Allen," Tex thought, "looks to be an inch taller." Tex would later write: "The initial flight of the airplane destined to change the travel habits of mankind was history."

He would take out the Dash-80 many times after that. In effect, he would wring it out, taking it up to 80 percent of its structural integrity. He would dive it, he would roll it, he would maneuver it in punishing ways. And always that euphemism, "structural integrity"—what it really means is that you hope you don't tear a goddamned wing off the thing.

A little more than two weeks went by before the Dash-80 nearly became a crumpled hunk of history. Tex was doing some high-speed braking tests at Boeing Field. Tremendous heat built up in the friction plates of the brake assembly in each wheel—with serious side effects of high temperature of the brake fluids. To cool off the brakes, Tex took the Dash-80 up to 25,000 feet with the landing gear down.

The Dash-80 had no thrust reversers, but the cooled-down brakes were thought to be enough to stop it.

So, on this especially nice afternoon, August 4, 1954, Tex brought the Dash-80 down on Runway 31 at Boeing Field. He applied the brakes. Nothing happened. Again. Nothing happened!

Jeeezus! No brakes! Runway 31 is disappearing behind him at a frightful rate. Here it comes, this 240,000-pound prototype beauty, one of a kind, a flying testbed, an airborne gene pool, the whole freaking company—and in a very few seconds they are going to have a smashed-up pile of jet technology and a couple of pulverized pilots. Do something!

Heaven is full of pilots who didn't "do something" in the one terrible moment when it had to be done. Tex did something. He went to the right rudder with his custom-built cowboy boots, the ones with an "80" engraved on them for demonstration flights and took the Dash-80 off the runway and onto soft ground. Anything to slow it down and avoid disaster.

The Dash-80 piled into a submerged hunk of concrete, hidden by weeds, and the nose gear, ripped from its mountings, dropped to the ground. Tex opened the cockpit window, got a look at the splayed nose gear and said, "Aw, shit!"

That was a setback, all right, but once more they got the plane fixed. Now the Dash-80 became a showpiece of the aviation world. Boeing was out selling it hard, which is to say it was selling the production model 707, and almost anything went.

The specter of Douglas was always there. Douglas had been a favorite of the airlines with its DC-3, DC- 4 and DC-6. Sometimes Boeing salesmen couldn't get a foot in the door. The DC-8, the Douglas version of the 707, was on the drawing boards; it was a paper airplane. The Dash-80 was a flying reality.

According to author Eugene Bauer, Boeing's sales director, Ralph Bell, lamented in a private communication: "Our prototype is our biggest asset, but it's also our biggest obstacle. Douglas has a rubber airplane. It's easy to stretch on paper."

On October 16, 1955, Boeing gathered up a cluster of VIPs, including Bill Allen. Johnston took them for a ride in the Dash-80 from Seattle to Andrews Air Force Base in Washington, D.C. The flight time was 3 hours and 48 minutes. The world had shrunk.

By early 1956, the Dash-80 had flown more than 100 demonstration flights with no fewer than 49 airline and government pilots trying their hands at the controls. (The insurance restriction had been lifted.) One of these was Howard Hughes, the eccentric owner of TWA.

Test pilot Brien Wygle drew the Hughes assignment. He flew the Dash-80 to Los Angeles, where he was prepared to brief the reclusive billionaire on jet flying. Hughes was a good enough pilot, to be sure, but he had never flown a big swept-wing jet.

Hughes showed up looking like somebody who would be turned away at the Bread of Life Mission. He was thin and gaunt, wore shoes without laces, no socks, a belt that missed trouser loops.

As Wygle says today, "The idea was to keep him happy-we were told not to upset the customer." Wygle and Hughes got along quite well as Brien briefed him on the techniques of jet flying. We flew it around for a while, then Hughes wanted to try a landing," Wygle recalls. "But on some things, he didn't respond."

One thing to which Hughes did not respond was Wygle's admonition not to land the Dash-80 too fast. The speed had to be kept down to 149 miles an hour on final, at or below flap speed. Anything above flap speed could damage the aircraft. Wygle recalls that, despite all the warnings, Hughes came in at 172 miles an hour.

A section of the flap tore off, a strip of metal about 18 inches wide and 8 feet long. It could easily have floated around for a while, then come down to slice some innocent citizen like a piece of sausage. Instead, the flap fragment came down on top of a car, although of all the thousands of cars parked around LAX, this one was the worst choice. It belonged to an employee of the Federal Aviation Administration.

When Wygle taxied the Dash-80 up to the TWA hangar, he had a committee of FAA officials waiting. Hughes did what he had always done well-he disappeared. He legged it into a waiting car and was gone, leaving Wygle to talk his way out of a serious jam. Brien had to take the blame—he was, after all, the pilot in command. He can smile about it today, but in those days, it was serious. "I got off with a fine of $500," he says.

The sales war continued between Douglas and Boeing. It was a buyer's market and the airlines were demanding. A shorter airplane? But of course. A longer airplane? Indeed, we can. A heavier airplane. Why not? The customer is always right.

The whole business, with its monumentally high stakes for Douglas and Boeing, was reminiscent of picky shoppers from Broadmoor and Laurelhurst ... a little longer, please. Just an inch wider, to be sure ... take it in a little at the waist.

Boeing sent its best engineering people out on the sales circuit—Schairer, Steiner, Beall, the lot of them. One flaw the airlines found in the Dash-80 was that it was slightly smaller in circumference than the proposed DC-8. The Boeing experts were all standing around and somebody said it would be a good idea to make the 707 four inches bigger around, one inch more than the DC-8. When he heard this, George Martin looked as though he were listening to the ravings of a lunatic. "But somehow it happened," Joe Sutter smiles. "The 707 got one inch bigger than the DC-8. It kind of grew that way." When a problem came up, Jack Steiner would say, "If we don't have a few problems we'll die of comfort."

The competition was fierce, and Sutter remembers that the experienced sales people at Douglas would refer derisively to Boeing's sales staff as "those rosy-cheeked engineers with wing-tipped shoes."

With the Dash-80 as a laboratory, Boeing set up what amounted to a faculty of flying instructors—Johnston, Waddell, Wygle, McMurry, Wallick and Layne. They would take up senior pilots of the leading airlines in the Dash-80 and break them in on swept-wing flying.

And of course, Douglas was wooing these same senior pilots and airline executives. The potential buyers would come and sit around in Santa Monica with great swatches of drawings, the proposed DC-8—spread out on a big table—and hear of the wonders of this great new airliner Douglas was building. And legend had it that you could almost hear some senior line pilot saying to himself, "Yes, you've got some nice drawings there. But I've flown the Dash-80 and I KNOW what that sonofabitch can do."

No more dramatic demonstration was given than the August day in 1955 when Tex Johnston slow-rolled the Dash-80 over Lake

Washington before 200,000 people watching the hydroplane races. Those 200,000 people were not the ones Tex wanted to impress. At the races that day were representatives from the International Air Transport Association (every airline company in the world included) and the Society of Aeronautical Engineers. "It was," Tex said later, "an assembly of the most important people in aviation."

Tex brought the Dash-80 down low over the lake, 200 feet above the water on a northeast heading. Over she went, and later Tex recalled, "I figgered I had their attention, so I did it again." On the second barrel roll, Bill Allen turned to Larry Bell, head of Bell Aircraft. "Give me one of your heart pills, I need it more than you do."

Bell laughed. Then he said, "Bill, you don't know Tex very well-he just sold your airplane for you."

When Allen called Tex into his office Monday morning, he demanded, "What did you think you were doing yesterday?"

"Selling your airplane," Tex said.

Allen didn't like Tex's risky sales technique, but the thin-faced high roller took some breathtaking chances on his own to put Boeing in the lead. In his book on Boeing, *Legend and Legacy*, Robert Serling describes a scene where Allen, Beall and Clyde Skeen were together in New York with Juan Trippe, then head of Pan American World Airways. Skeen was given the job of crunching numbers for Trippe and then he announced the price of a 707: "Four-point-two-eight million, including engines but no spares."

As Serling describes it, Trippe turned to Allen and said: "Well, Bill, down the hall in another room I have Donald Douglas Senior and Junior … their price is three-point-nine million."

The high-roller never missed a beat. "I think," he said, smoothly, "that Mr. Skeen is wrong. Our price is three-point-nine million."

But matching the Douglas price didn't help. Pan Am announced it was buying 25 DC-8s, but only 20 707s. The sales war went on. Beall went to Paris to sell the 707 to Air France. Joe Sutter sold four beefed-up 707s to Sabena.

In the early going Boeing sold 10 planes to Air France, 30 to American, five to Braniff and four to Continental. Douglas countered with six to Delta, 18 to Eastern, four to JAL and eight to KLM. The running score was posted in front-page headlines of both Seattle papers. The good news: "Boeing Sells 23 Jets to Pan Am." The bad news: "Douglas DC-8 Order Goes to SAS."

By the fall of 1957 it was all good news. The rosy-cheeked engineers with wing-tipped shoes were winning the race to dominate the skies. In 1957 Boeing took the lead in sales—145 jet airliners sold to 124 for the DC-8. As Robert Serling recorded: "It was a lead the company was never to relinquish."

By the end of the first jet decade, according to Serling, "the 707 single-handedly had ended the Douglas domination of the world's commercial airplane market." The Dash-80's progeny added up to more than 1,000 707s of various configurations: it was used as the president's Air Force One; it was produced as an AWACs military plane; its cousin, the C-135 tanker, still is in service today. When they stopped building 707s early in 1991, some 400 of them were still in service.

What does she look like today, this grandmother of Boeing's entire family of jets? Why, she looks like … an aging show-biz beauty. In her time, she has had facelifts, slimming diets, girdles, breast implants, new costumes, revised innards-the very picture of an aging star out to preserve her beauty and enhance her function.

I rode in her once. The Dash-80 was making a short ceremonial flight from Boeing up to Paine Field near Everett. Climbing aboard was Tex Johnston, now in his late 70s, still wearing a big Stetson and handmade cowboy boots. "They got this funny rule," he drawled, "that I'm too old to fly this thing. I might even be too old to ride in it."

On the forward bulkhead is a placard that says "Experimental. Passengers notified that this aircraft does not comply with Federal safety regulations for standard aircraft."

Standard aircraft, indeed. The Dash-8O now has 727 flight controls and a horizontal stabilizer from a 707- 720. The original engines were replaced by more powerful JT3D-l engines. Its flap system was modified. Even the wings have been changed. If you stand outside the Dash-80 and view the tail section, you will see the markings where they once installed a rear engine for 727 feasibility tests.

In her time, the Dash-80 carried tons of experimental radio and technical gear. During tests she was modified, patched, changed and rechanged dozens of times. She was conceived and designed to withstand abuse as her legacy to jets of the future. "Structural integrity."

Yes, she was a tough bird, this lady.

She has been flown by hundreds of pilots from dozens of countries. She has been flown by company executives, the head of the U.S. Air Force, high-ranking officers, presidents and VIPs of all sorts. She was once flown by the legendary Charles A. Lindbergh.

The Dash-80 has been systematically tortured, asked to do the nearly impossible; she has withstood spine-jolting landings, suffered brake fires, been flown near the speed of sound, and survived several 10,000- feet-per-minute demonstration dives. Through it all she was a fecund, productive brood mare for Boeing jets that fly the skies of all the world.

Long ago, when the B-47, the B-52 and the Dash-80 were being designed and built, the young lions at Boeing foresaw a "family" of jets, a veritable stable of aircraft—many variations of each model. George Schairer, Jack Steiner, Maynard Pennell, Joe Sutter and all the rest—they knew what was coming. Bill Allen had rolled the dice for them, and because he was lucky—and right—the world was forever changed.

Out of the Dash-80 came the 727 tri jet, the twin engine 737, the giant 747 and ultimately, because of the company's enormous background in jet design, the 757, the 767 and the revolutionary 777.

When Tex Johnston poured the coals to the Dash- 80 back in 1955, crossing the continent in 3 hours and 48 minutes, the revolution in air transportation had begun. The time from Paris to New York had shrunk from 12 hours and 30 minutes to barely more than 6 hours. The time from Seattle to Tokyo or Saigon or Singapore was cut by half.

For Seattle the shorter travel times made all the difference. Seattle had always been known as "a city that was a long way from anyplace," but that no longer was true. As Tex Johnston said, "We have shrunk the world by a factor of two."

For a long time during the 1950s, Seattle was known as Dullsburg, Northwest, a city of contentment and blue laws and more rain than seemed absolutely necessary. It was an isolated place, where Easterners (some of them) literally thought you could take a taxi to Alaska. But all of that changed when Boeing—meaning Seattle—ushered in the jet age. Not only did William Allen's willingness to gamble put his company on the "do pass" line, but his winning gamble put this city on the center stage of the world.

Seattle became "Boeing's town, the place where they build those jets." In sometimes derisive terms Seattle was called "a company town," and there was truth in this. But if Seattle was Boeing, it was also true that Boeing was Seattle. The people who launched the world into jet air travel lived here; they were part of the city.

At airports all over the world people began to see these sleek, swift progenies of the Dash-80. And people came to learn that these jets were not made in Toledo or Houston. These jets were made in Seattle.

"Boeing is the world's most successful aerospace company," writes Robert Serling. "In 1990 alone, its jets carried more people than live in the earth's 100 largest cities—675 million, the equivalent of 12 percent of the world's population." Sixty percent of the jets operated by the world's airlines today are built by Boeing.

The first passenger-carrying 707, bought by Pan Am, was put into service in October 1958. We didn't know it then, but the 707 was going to blow our cover. Those of us who liked a smallish, provincial town, low-rise and even low-self-esteem, were in for a jarring change. When the jets came, millions more people began to fly. From the beginning, jet airliner travel became a roaring commercial success. More than 1,000 707 jets were built; they were sold to 76 different companies, here and abroad. They have carried more than 706 million passengers.

From the moment he flew in the first Boeing swept-wing jet, the B-47, Bill Allen knew it was time to go for broke. He decided to make all other air transport obsolete in 1952 when he risked bankruptcy for Boeing—when he turned loose these incredibly young and gifted airplane technocrats and told them, in effect, to go out and beat the world.

They, too, had structural integrity.

When the 707 blew our cover, it changed the way we lived. People came here from everywhere-from all over the nation, from Asia, Africa, South America and Europe. Within a few years, Seattle became an entirely different place. With the city's discovery, the arts flourished, restaurants got better, buildings became taller; with jet travel came major league sports, better music, better theater. Traveling to Seattle became as easy as boarding a bus from San Francisco to San Jose, from Manhattan to Buffalo.

Where are they now, the young lions who shrunk the world? Why, they are all around you. Many have passed away, to be sure, but many of the great ones, men like Jack Steiner, Joe Sutter, Maynard Pennell and George Schairer—indeed, hundreds more—live here in comfortable retirement. All but one or two of those great old pilots-swashbuckling Tex Johnston, Lew Wallick, Brien Wygle, Jack Waddell, Jim Gannett, Tom Layne—the great jet jockeys who taught the piston—bound airline pilots how to fly a new, faster, safer, more comfortable airplane are still here.

The Dash-80 was turned over to the Smithsonian Institution's Aeronautics and Space Museum in 1972. The Smithsonian designated it as "one of the ten most important airplanes ever built." But the Smithsonian had no space to display it in Washington, D.C.

For 18 years the Dash-80 baked in the desert sun at Davis-Monthan Air Base near Tucson. It was the Dash-80's indignity to be abandoned in that aircraft graveyard. But a crew of Boeing experts, several of them retired volunteers, went down and retrieved the Dash-80. They flew her back to Boeing, where she has been restored to her former splendor. If you drive out Airport Way and get near the Museum of Flight, you'll see her parked there on the tarmac—the true icon of world jet travel, yellow and brown, ancient, of course, but always beautiful.

Bill Allen died in retirement, at his Highlands home on October 29, 1987. His career at Boeing spanned 47 years. The high roller was a legend in the world of aviation.

Time is never warped; it is always moving, much too quickly, faster than we realize. Passing time makes generations obsolete.

Once, a few years ago, I did a retrospective magazine story on Tex Johnston. Tex had loaned me part of his picture collection to use for illustrations. The editor was a nice woman in her 30s. We had the pictures spread out on a table—pictures of Johnston and the B-47, the B-52 and his great slow roll in the Dash-80 over Lake Washington. "And here," I said, pointing, "is a picture of Bill Allen."

She looked up in honest, wide-eyed wonderment. "Who was Bill Allen?" she said.

About the Author

Emmett Watson was a fixture in Seattle journalism for more than half a century, first as a sports writer fo the Seatle Star and then as a columinist for the *Seattle Post-Intelligencer* and the *Seattle Times*. Orphaned shortly after his birth in 1918, Wstson was raised by John and Elizabeth Watson, of West Seattle.

He initially pursued a career in basebll, bur proved more successful describing games than playing them. He scored his first international scoop by revealing the suicide of author Ernest Hemingway in 1961, and later entertained generations with his pithy commentaries of Seattle's changing social landscape. A paladin with a pen, Watson stood for Lesser Seattle against Greater Seattle, and delighted in puncturing the pompositites of local Babbits and self-appointed civic Boosters. He died of post-surgical complications on May 11, 2001.

About the Author

Emmett Watson was a fixture in Seattle journalism for more than half a century, first as a sports writer fo the Seatle Star and then as a columinist for the *Seattle Post-Intelligencer* and the *Seattle Times*. Orphaned shortly after his birth in 1918, Wstson was raised by John and Elizabeth Watson, of West Seattle.

He initially pursued a career in basebll, bur proved more successful describing games than playing them. He scored his first international scoop by revealing the suicide of author Ernest Hemingway in 1961, and later entertained generations with his pithy commentaries of Seattle's changing social landscape. A paladin with a pen, Watson stood for Lesser Seattle against Greater Seattle, and delighted in puncturing the pompositites of local Babbits and self-appointed civic Boosters. He died of post-surgical complications on May 11, 2001.